THE FOUNDER'S MENTALITY

HOW TO OVERCOME THE
PREDICTABLE CRISES OF GROWTH

THE FOUNDER'S MENTALITY

CHRIS ZOOK & JAMES ALLEN

Harvard Business Review Press
Boston, Massachusetts

Printed in the United States of America

20 19 18 17 16 15 14

Library of Congress Cataloging-in-Publication Data

Names: Zook, Chris, 1951- author. | Allen, James, 1960- author.
Title: The founder's mentality : how to overcome the predictable crises of growth / Chris Zook, James Allen.
Description: Boston, Massachusetts : Harvard Business Review Press, [2016]
Identifiers: LCCN 2015049494 (print) | LCCN 2016004772 (ebook) | ISBN 9781633691162 (hardback) | ISBN 9781633691179 ()
Subjects: LCSH: Corporations—Growth. | Industrial management. | Corporate profits. | Strategic planning. | Leadership. | BISAC: BUSINESS & ECONOMICS / Strategic Planning. | BUSINESS & ECONOMICS / Management. | BUSINESS & ECONOMICS / Leadership.
Classification: LCC HD2746 .Z658 2016 (print) | LCC HD2746 (ebook) | DDC 658.4/06—dc23
LC record available at http://lccn.loc.gov/2015049494

The paper used in this publication meets the requirements of the American National Standard for Permanence of Paper for Publications and Documents in Libraries and Archives Z39.48-1992.

CONTENTS

THE FOUNDER'S MENTALITY

INTRODUCTION

The Paradox of Growth

Growth creates complexity, and complexity is the silent killer of growth. This paradox explains why only about one company in nine has sustained more than a minimum level of profitable growth during the past decade, and why 85 percent of executives blame internal factors for their shortfall, not external ones beyond their control.[1] The roots of sustained performance start deep inside, and they are predictable.

If you look carefully, you can always find two intertwining plot lines in the story of any business success or failure. The first, and the most visible, is the external story. This is the narrative that plays out in the marketplace in the form of quarterly earnings, returns to shareholders, market share shifts, and profitable growth. This is the story that is easiest to track, and it's the one that most people—boards of directors, investors, the press, the public—choose to follow. It's a story about how a company wins on the outside by serving the customer better than its competitors.

The second story plays out *inside* a company. It's much less visible. It's the story of building the business, expanding and retaining a quality workforce, strengthening the culture, upgrading the systems, learning from experience, adapting the business model, holding down costs, and mobilizing the people to carry it all out perfectly, again and again.

Some companies excel externally but are troubled internally; others are troubled externally but excel internally. Ultimately, though, companies have to excel in both arenas if they want to succeed. The plot lines have to converge. You can't sustain profitable growth in a competitive market if you're a disaster internally, and you can't maintain a high-performance culture internally for long if you're failing in the marketplace.

We've written four books about how to win the external strategy game, starting with *Profit from the Core*. This book is different. It's about the inside game of strategy. It's about how companies, both young and mature, can avoid what we've identified as the three internal crises of growth.

The Predictable Crises of Growth

Each of the three crises we've identified occurs at a different phase in a company's life.

The first crisis, *overload*, refers to the internal dysfunction and loss of external momentum that management teams of young, fast-growing companies experience as they try to rapidly scale their businesses.

The second crisis, *stall-out*, refers to the sudden slowdown that many successful companies suffer as their rapid growth gives rise to layers of organizational complexity and dilutes the clear mission that once gave the company its focus and energy. Stall-out is a disorienting time for a company: the accelerator pedal of growth no longer responds as it used to, and faster, younger competitors are starting to gain ground. Most companies that stall out never fully recover.

The third crisis, *free fall*, is the most existentially threatening. A company in free fall has completely stopped growing in its core market, and its business model, until recently the reason for its success, suddenly no longer seems viable. Time feels scarce for a company in free fall. The management team often feels it has lost control. It can't identify the root causes of the crisis, and it doesn't know what levers to pull to escape it.

These three crises represent the riskiest and most stressful periods for businesses that have made it successfully through their start-up and early-growth phases. The good news is these crises are predictable and often avoidable. The killers of growth that these crises contain can be anticipated and even turned into a constructive reason for change.

The Founder's Mentality

Our insights in this book are based on a simple but profound truth. Despite their many differences, most companies that achieve sustainable growth share a common set of motivating attitudes and behaviors that can usually be traced back to a bold, ambitious founder who got it right the first time around. The companies that have grown profitably to scale, while maintaining the internal traits that got them there in the first place, often consider themselves insurgents, waging war on their industry and its standards on behalf of an underserved customer, or creating an entirely new industry altogether. Such companies possess a clear sense of mission and focus that everyone in the company can understand and relate to (in contrast with the average company, where only two employees in five say they have any idea what the company stands for).[2] Companies run in this way have the special ability to foster employees' deep feelings of personal responsibility (in contrast with the average company, where a recent Gallup survey shows that only 13 percent of employees say they are emotionally engaged with their company).[3] They abhor complexity, bureaucracy, and anything that gets in the way of the clean execution of strategy. They are obsessed with the details of the business and celebrate the employees at the front line, who deal directly with customers. Together, these attitudes and behaviors constitute a frame of mind that is one of the great and most undervalued secrets of business success.

We call it *the founder's mentality.*

The founder's mentality constitutes a key source of competitive advantage for younger companies going up against larger, better-endowed incumbents, and it consists of three main traits: an insurgent's mission, an owner's mindset, and obsession with the front line. In their purest expression, these traits can be found in companies that are founder-led, or where the clear influence of the founder still remains in the principles, norms, and values that guide employees' day-to-day decisions and behaviors.

In our analyses, surveys, and interviews (see the sidebar later in this chapter, "How We Did the Research"), we've found a consistently strong relationship between the traits of the founder's mentality in companies of all kinds—not just start-ups—and their ability to sustain performance in the marketplace, in the stock market, and against their peers. Since 1990, we've found that the returns to shareholders in public companies where the founder is still involved are three times higher than in other companies (see figure I-1).[4] The most consistent high performers exhibit the attributes of the founder's mentality four to five times more than

FIGURE I-1

Founder-led companies outperform the rest

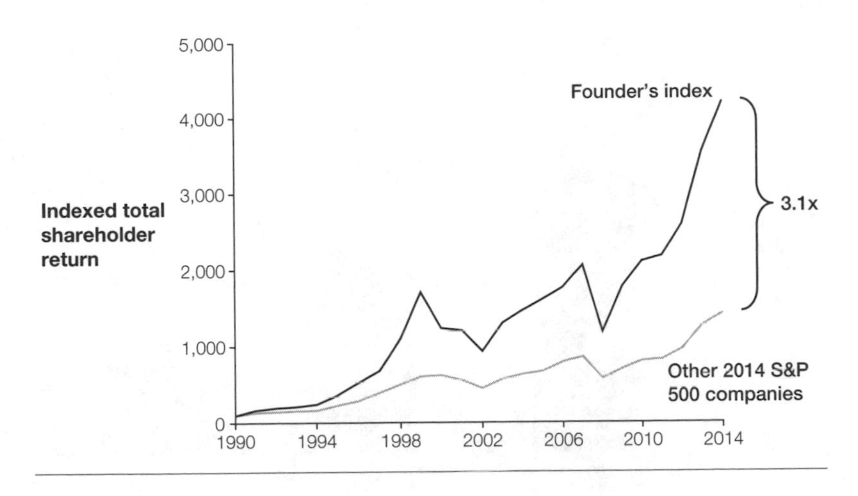

the worst performers.[5] Furthermore, we've determined that of the roughly one in ten companies that achieve a decade of sustained and profitable growth, nearly two in three are governed by the founder's mentality. These are all remarkable numbers.

All too often, however, companies lose the founder's mentality as they become larger. The pursuit of growth and scale adds organizational complexity, piles on processes and systems, dilutes the sense of insurgency, and creates challenges in maintaining the original level of talent. These sorts of deep, subtle internal problems, in turn, lead to deterioration on the outside. Figure I-2, based on a global survey we have conducted of 325 executives, shows the decreasing degree to which company leaders perceive the founder's mentality at work in their own company, depending on its size.

How else to explain the disappointments of companies that once dominated their business and seemed to have everything—growing markets, massive investable funds, proprietary technologies, best-known brands, leadership in their channels? In the

FIGURE I-2

Executives perceive a decline in the founder's mentality with size

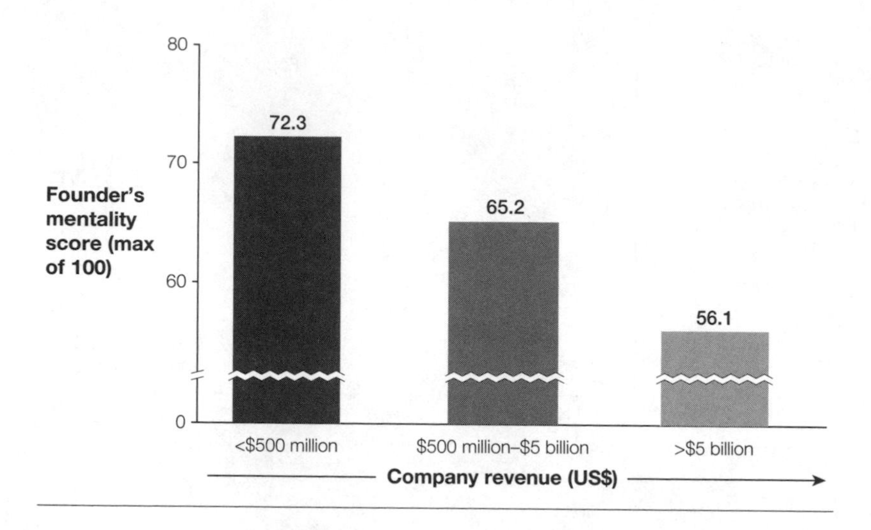

1990s, for example, Nokia rocketed to the top of the handset market. During that decade, we estimate, the company captured more than 90 percent of the market's global profits and seemed poised to maintain its leadership for years to come. It even was putting in place many of the elements for next-generation smartphones: it had developed some of the earliest small-touchscreen technology, was the global leader in selling tiny cameras, had learned how to distribute music, and was one of the first companies to offer free e-mail on its phones. Yet somehow, overloaded by its own growth and blinded by its burgeoning organizational complexity, the company failed to capitalize on its advantages and take the lead in developing next-generation phones, despite calls from some of its own engineers to do just that.

None of this stemmed from a lack of resources or opportunity. Nokia sat on top of one of the biggest growth markets the world had ever seen, and on top of one of the biggest piles of cash in history. But instead of thinking like an insurgent and investing in the future, it gave out 40 percent dividends and used its cash to buy back large quantities of its own stock. Within just a few years, Apple, Samsung, and soon Google had seized the smartphone market, and Nokia, once a model of innovation and insurgent-style thinking, was in steep decline. A board member, when interviewed about what happened, pointed to internal factors, not competitive moves, and concluded simply, "We were too slow to act."[6]

In our studies of growth crises, we've come across a plethora of companies like Nokia—companies that seemed on the outside to have everything (market position, brand, technology, customer base, enormous financial resources) but ultimately lost it all in shocking fashion, because of how they failed to play the internal game. But we've also encountered many remarkable and inspiring stories of the opposite nature (several that you will read in this book)—companies that seemed on the outside to have no hope but that were revived by leaders who virtually refounded the company from the inside.

One such company is DaVita, which has transformed itself since 1999 from a company that seemed headed for bankruptcy into one of the best-performing health-care companies in the United States today. Since Kent Thiry took over as CEO and publicly disclosed the full extent of the company's troubles, its stock price (adjusted for splits) has increased by a hundred times and its market value has grown from almost zero to $15 billion. Thiry, still CEO nearly sixteen years later, engineered this transformation by first reenergizing the company on the inside with the founder's mentality; later in this book, we'll explore in detail how.

How We Did the Research

We've put years of research and analysis into this book. We began with the observation that profitable growth globally was becoming more challenging and more fleeting, and that barely one in ten companies achieved it over a decade. We confirmed this observation by developing a database at Bain & Company of all public companies in the global stock markets, tracked during the past twenty-five years. We then looked at the list of companies that were the most successful at maintaining profitable growth over the long term and found that they were disproportionately companies with a superior ability both to stay focused on the opportunities in and around their core business and to seek new growth primarily by adapting and extending their core. When we looked closely at this list of super adaptors, we found that they were most often companies where the founder was still running the business (like Oracle, Haier, or L Brands) or was still involved on the board of directors, or, most importantly, where the focus and principles of how to operate that the founder once put in place still endured, because he or she had gotten it nearly right the first time (like IKEA or Enterprise Rent-A-Car). We calculated the returns to shareholders in companies with these founder connections, analyzed the attributes of the most enduring successes, and discovered that this hypothesis was borne out in spades. To find out why, we went into the field.

We first spoke to over one hundred executives around the world about the barriers to growth they perceived, and, at the same time, launched an initiative at Bain for high-growth companies now called the Founder's Mentality 100 (FM100). Initially, the FM100 focused on young companies in developing markets that generally had attained well over $200 million in size and had promising long-term growth prospects. Most of the executives we talked to in our travels and in our FM100 workshops told us that the root causes of their failure to grow were internal, not external.

We then invested in several surveys of global executives to confirm and understand those barriers to growth. One survey involved 325 executives in a cross section of businesses; another involved our FM100 executives and their teams, across fifty-six companies. Each produced similar results: the executives we talked to identified internal barriers as the root cause of many of their growth challenges, though where they put the most emphasis naturally varied by age and stage of development.

We then went in pursuit of the success factors that make up the founder's mentality. We did this through a series of interviews worldwide with executives and founders, and through a database we built of two hundred companies, their performance, and their dominant practices, as assessed by an expert who knew each company well. Three sets of hard-edged practices and underlying attitudes, often tracing back to the way the founder set up the company, emerged consistently. We confirmed and discussed these further in our FM100 workshops, in discussions with our industry specialists at Bain & Company, and through dozens of more formal interviews with senior executives and especially founders. People everywhere were very generous with their time, and all were keenly interested in the topic. This allowed us to define the elements of the founder's mentality and begin to understand their practical use in companies facing the three most pressing crises of growth.

Finally, we conducted a range of deeper case studies, focusing on companies that seemed to maintain the founder's mentality over a long time, companies that had lost and regained it, and companies that had never really had it. We chose examples spanning geographies, industries, and maturity in search of the "how" behind the "what." We dug deep into public data, got privileged access to all sorts of executives, and, above all, intimately familiarized ourselves with the stories of a set of remarkable founders who continue to amaze and inspire us.

Why This Book Now

Overload, stall-out, and free fall may all be predictable crises, but we've discovered that good solutions exist for overcoming them. And overcoming them is vital: on average, more than 80 percent of the major swings in value in companies' lives can be traced to the decisions and actions the companies take—or do not take—at these three moments of crisis.[7]

Not only is overcoming these crises vital, it has also never been more urgent. That's because business life cycles—and the metabolisms of whole industries—have been speeding up dramatically. Consider this: on average, new companies that reach *Fortune* 500 scale today are doing so more than two times faster than just two decades ago, and the fastest—the world record holders for scaling—are exceeding prior records by a wide margin.[8] Another indicator that young companies are achieving market power sooner: in 40 percent of the competitive arenas, the strongest company—that is, the company with the biggest share of industry profits and, thus, the greatest ability to reinvest—is no longer the largest.[9] Advances in technology, and the increasing shift in value toward services and software where scale is less important, are eroding the advantages of size. As a result, young insurgents are becoming a threat to incumbents earlier than ever. And here's the other part of the story: once these insurgents themselves become incumbents, they are stalling out more often and more suddenly, and are having a harder time recovering than ever before.[10]

This double whammy of faster growth early in life and faster stall-out later in life has resulted in a more rapid reordering of strategic positions in many industries, and has caused leaders and followers in many markets to change places with frightening speed (see figure I-3). Take the airline industry: a well-established, capital-intensive industry with high barriers to entry and no totally disruptive technology. This is not the kind of industry in which, traditionally, you would expect to witness a major strategic reordering. But that's precisely what has happened in the past couple of decades. If you look at a list of the top-twenty airlines by value in 1999 and then compare that with today's list, you find that the industry leaders have churned by more than half, that bankruptcies have been common, and that roughly half of the companies that were on the list sixteen years ago are not even independent companies today. The airlines that are the most valuable in the world, such as Air China, didn't even make the top twenty in 1999. And this phenomenon is by no means unique to the airlines. Well over half of executives from across all industries say that their main competitor in five years will be a different company than it is today.[11] It is a testament to the speed at which young companies can grow and become forces in their industries.

FIGURE I-3

Increasing speed of scaling and declining

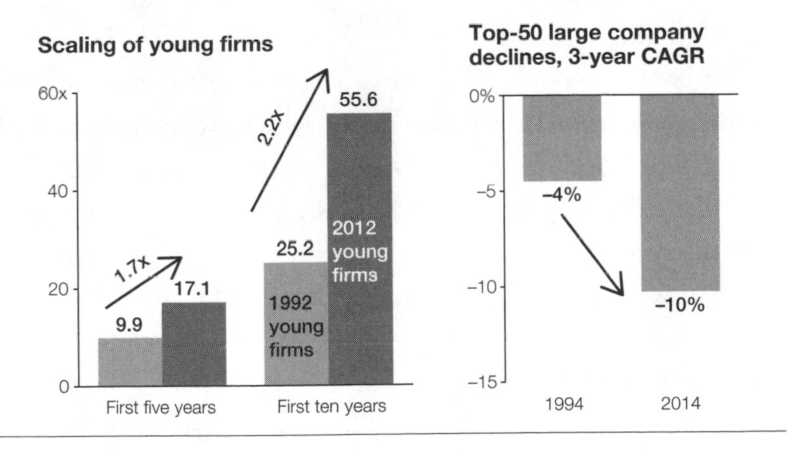

What You Will Get from This Book

We've written this book with a very practical goal in mind: to help companies achieve sustainable success by navigating a safe passage through the internal crises of growth. We believe that there are three types of readers who will benefit the most from the insights and ideas in this book. The first are members of leadership teams, including founders themselves, who are grappling directly with the challenges of achieving their growth targets. This includes all those in the organization who report to the senior team, those aspiring to greater leadership roles in the companies, and those in the middle layers who are responsible for implementing strategy and managing communication between upper and lower levels. The second type is the investor who is trying to assess a company's growth prospects and the difficulty level of the challenges it will face on the way. The third is the board member who is concerned about the growth momentum or prospects of a company and wants a research-based means of asking the tough questions about preparedness for future challenges and barriers. All three types of readers—the leaders, the investors, and the board members—will find value in our research, our conclusions, and the stories we use to illustrate them.

This book is about how best to scale a business that has moved successfully beyond the start-up period while also maintaining the energy, focus, and obsessive attention to the customer that were the reasons for its initial success. It is different, in other words, from the recent tsunami of literature on the secrets of start-ups. For that, we refer readers to books such as *The Lean Startup* by Eric Ries or *Zero to One* by Peter Thiel. This book is also different from those that focus on the early start-up dynamics of founder- and family-led companies. Readers interested in that topic should start with *The Founder's Dilemmas* by Noam Wasserman, which is perhaps the definitive work on this topic, and go from there.

We have devoted our careers to helping leaders of businesses find their next wave of profitable growth. Sometimes we've helped young companies as they struggle with an overload of growth opportunities, sometimes we've helped mature companies find ways to avoid stall-out, and sometimes we've helped companies in free fall completely redefine their business model. We look back on these experiences with enormous respect for the leaders in the center of the arena who must personally confront these challenges. We offer the ideas in this book with great humility but also confidence and optimism. They don't represent an elixir. But they're based on lessons we've learned from carefully studying some of the best-performing companies and leaders in the world, and we strongly believe that most companies facing growth crises can apply the principles of the founder's mentality, as we define it in this book, to greatly improve their odds of success.

How This Book Is Organized

This book is built around the attributes of the founder's mentality, and how they each can help management teams of all sorts understand and address the three predictable crises of growth.

In chapter 1, we'll define the founder's mentality, show how it interacts with the process of scaling, and introduce the three predictable crises of growth. In chapter 2, we'll explore the forces that trigger these crises and will demonstrate their role in creating or destroying value through the life of a company. We'll then devote a chapter to each of the three crises: overload in chapter 3, stall-out in chapter 4, and free fall in chapter 5. Finally, in chapter 6, we'll look at the idea of *scale insurgency* as a model of how to achieve sustainable growth, and we'll conclude with a discussion of the lessons that our work on the founder's mentality holds for leaders at all levels of an organization.

Research is the bedrock on which we've based this book, but stories are how we've built it up: stories that we feel reflect the most practical ideas and lessons from our research, stories of how leaders have overcome the crises of growth, stories of disappointments that proved to be avoidable, stories of renewal. We've observed some of the world's most effective leadership teams in action, and they've talked candidly to us about what has worked for them and what hasn't. Drawing on that access, we'll provide you with an in-depth look at what the founder's mentality is, and we'll show you how companies of all sorts have overcome the paradox of growth by continually using the founder's mentality as the touchstone for everything they do. Our hope is that this book will empower leaders everywhere to infuse the founder's mentality throughout their own companies, and to control the destiny of their companies in an uncertain future by mastering the internal game of strategy. Ultimately, this book is about addressing the pressing needs of the future—a future that more than ever rewards speed, open-mindedness, human motivation, and adaptability.

Let's begin with the story of one of the great founders of our time.

1

The Founder's Mentality

The Key to Achieving Sustainable Growth

Every great business founder has an origin story to tell. For Leslie Wexner, that story began one day in 1963, when, at the age of twenty-five, he concluded that he could create a retail business that would achieve better results than the one run by his parents.

Wexner had been born and raised in Dayton, Ohio, the son of a Russian-Jewish immigrant father who had emigrated to avoid persecution. His father, Harry Wexner, who never learned how to write, had worked his way up at a Chicago department store from package wrapper to store walker to window trimmer to manager; his mother, Bella Wexner, who had started at the Lazarus department store as an administrative assistant, had risen to become the youngest buyer in the store. Together, despite working long hours, they had never made more than $9,000 a year. "We had absolutely no money," Wexner recalled. "Zero." In 1951, hoping to do better on their own, they opened a small store, with a storefront only thirteen feet wide. They named it Leslie's, after their son. But their situation didn't improve much.

This nagged at Wexner, who had studied business as an undergraduate at Ohio State University in Columbus. How was it that his parents, who were always working so hard, hadn't managed to get further ahead in life? Part of the answer came to him after college, when he was helping out at the store and came across a set of invoices. As he studied them, he realized that his parents had filled their store with big-ticket items that sold with lower net margins, such as dresses and coats. What were selling at higher profitability and keeping the store afloat, however, were the average-priced items, such as shirts, skirts, and pants. To Wexner, the solution was obvious: sell more of the merchandise with the best economics. Wexner enthusiastically took this idea to his father, who, less than receptive, told him to get a job.

So he did. Convinced that he could succeed, Wexner founded his own business: a specialized clothing store for women at the Kingsdale Shopping Center, in Upper Arlington, Ohio, that, in contrast with his parents' general-merchandise strategy, would stock only a limited selection of clothing and focus on what sold best. He called his store The Limited.

To launch his business, Wexner turned for help to his Aunt Ida, who lent him $5,000 as collateral. With that money, he got a $10,000 bank loan and set to work. This was no tentative venture. Convinced it would succeed, he signed a lease for a second store and ratcheted up his liabilities more than $1 million even before he opened his first store. He was all in and had a powerfully personal sense of what was at stake. "With $1 million of debt and no equity," he said, "I felt that a bear was chasing me and would eat me if I stood still for a second," adding, "If it didn't work, I would be the most notorious bankruptcy in Ohio."

Receipts in The Limited's first year were $160,000, not enough to reduce Wexner's anxiety but enough to keep him going a bit longer. Despite his fragile finances, he embarked on an ambitious plan of growth, opening a new store in each of the next five years; each succeeded, thanks in large part to his force of will. "I felt that I could win by always outworking my competitors," he said. "If they worked twelve hours a day, I would work sixteen. I was determined to make sure that everyone left the store with a reason to come back. I thought, '*We do not have much money, we do not have many stores, but at least I can be enthusiastic.*' You can describe it as passion for success."

Wexner also succeeded in his early years by developing an unrelenting focus on the front line. "I treated each customer as a friend," he said. If they didn't like what they'd bought from him, he decided, they could bring it back for a refund, not a common practice at the time, and one his father told him was crazy. But he did it anyway. From the start, too, Wexner imbued The Limited with a sense of personality and purpose. The Limited, he believed, should exist to serve the needs of a very precise kind of customer: a smart, strong, independent modern woman, typified by Jenny Cavalleri, the beloved character played by Ali McGraw in *Love Story*. "I built my store around an image of a woman like her," he said, "and what she would want to wear."

In 1969, with six successful stores in operation, Wexner took another unconventional risk: he decided to take The Limited public with an intrastate offering, in order to provide his employees with real equity that would make them share his owner's mindset. People ridiculed the decision at the time, but it turned out to be a good one. If you had invested $1,000 in The Limited when it went public, your stake today would be worth $60 million.

Today, L Brands, as Wexner now calls his company, employs a hundred thousand people. Running the company poses all sorts of complex management challenges, but as Wexner and his management team confront them, they remain as focused as ever on their core mission and ideals. "I knew that we needed to become a big company in order to be able to compete economically," he said. "But above all, I wanted to build a good company with a special purpose and clear values." In working toward that goal, Wexner learned an important lesson by reading *Making Movies* by Sidney Lumet. "You have to think of all of the creative talents when you make a movie," he said, "like designers, actors, producers, directors, costume designers, musicians. Yet when you see a great movie, it's cohesive, as if one person did it all. Great brands have that cohesive point of personality and require attention to coherent detail."

In the decades since he founded The Limited, Wexner's businesses have moved from success to success. Today, as the head of L Brands, he is the longest-serving CEO of any major *Fortune* 500 company in North America. Over the course of the past fifty-two years, he has made a success of not only The Limited but also Express, Bath & Body Works, Abercrombie & Fitch, Henri Bendel, La Senza, and—the jewel in his crown today—Victoria's Secret. In doing so, he has produced a return of nearly 20 percent per year for his shareholders, and L Brands has a market value of roughly $28 billion. In large part, he has succeeded because he thinks and acts like an insurgent. "When you stop to smell the roses," he said, "is when you get hit by a truck. Success does not naturally beget success. The hardest thing to do is to keep your edge and stay on your game as you succeed and grow. Consequently, I refuse to accept the fact that I am mature, or that the business is mature. As soon as you accept that, you begin to die."

The Founder's Mentality: Three Defining Traits

Les Wexner and his L Brands team exude the founder's mentality. They live and breathe their insurgent mission. No matter how big their companies have become, they remain obsessed with the front line, always aware that the details there make all the difference. And theirs is an owner's mindset, a powerful sense of responsibility for all of their employees, customers, products, and decisions.

These three traits—*the insurgent mission*, *the front-line obsession*, and *the owner's mindset*—are key traits of the founder's mentality, and our research shows that assiduously cultivating them leads to success (see figure 1-1).

In the following section, we'll describe how three founders instilled those traits in their companies during the early days

FIGURE 1-1

The defining traits of the founder's mentality

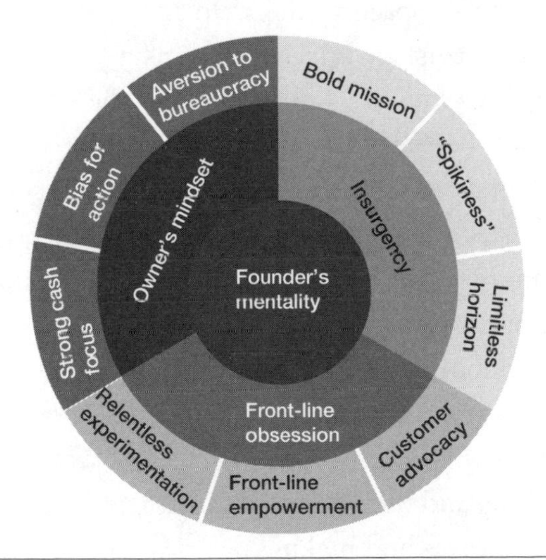

and then maintained them as the companies became large. Our point here is basic but important: the founder's mentality does not have to wane over time, as companies age, nor does it have to disappear when a founder retires or dies; it can help companies of all ages and sizes achieve sustainable growth. We have chosen to focus here on the stories of founders simply because, in those stories, we've found the purest and most enduring expression of the founder's mentality.

An Insurgent Mission

The first element of the founder's mentality is the sense of an insurgent mission. As we mentioned in our introduction, some of the most successful founders have likened the start-up phase to waging war against an industry on behalf of underserved customers—this is why, in the early years, Wexner held company meetings in what he called his "war room." Others have described their purpose as redefining the rules of their industry. And still others see the insurgency as creating totally new markets, as SpaceX is doing in space travel, or perhaps as Netflix is doing in on-demand television. Typically, the insurgent mission derives from a company's founder, but in many of the really sustainable businesses, it ultimately takes hold at every level and can far outlast the founder. Let's look more closely at the components of insurgency, using the example of Yonghui Superstores, a rapidly growing founder-led grocery business in China that is challenging larger rivals, even Walmart.

Yonghui's founders, Zhang Xuansong and Zhang Xuanning, are brothers who grew up in humble circumstances in rural Fujian in the southeast corner of China. Their father was a contractor in the local village, and their mother made extra money at home by processing tea leaves and making pastries. The brothers grew up helping their mother do her work. Inspired by this experience, in the mid-1980s, they founded a small local grocery business selling local beer and common packaged foods. The business quickly expanded to five small locations. Then, in 1999, something happened that changed everything for the brothers: China got its first hypermarkets.

These new stores were giant by Chinese standards, spreading over more than ten thousand square meters, and they carried packaged goods and produce: the traditional grocery profile. Intrigued, the brothers began studying how the stores were run and gradually decided that they could do it better. They saw, for example, that the hypermarkets were purchasing fresh produce from distributors and earning about 17 percent gross margin. Why not eliminate the middle layers of distribution, they thought, and just purchase directly from the farmers? That would allow them to more than double the gross margin while also forging partnerships with local farmers and bringing produce faster and fresher to customers. They began to imagine a hybrid: stores that were big, clean, and air-conditioned, like the hypermarkets, but that also developed a supply chain directly to the farmers that allowed them to sell lower-cost, higher-quality produce. They decided to give it a try, and in 2000 they opened their first store, the Yonghui Pingxi Fresh Product Supermarket. It was an instant success.

As they prospered, they opened more stores, which allowed them to further increase their supply-chain advantage. For instance, they were willing to pay the farmers in cash, something the large chains were not willing to do. They also developed relationships with the local farmers to take all of their produce and offer guaranteed minimum reimbursement in years of bumper crops—a huge concern for rural farmers.

In everything they did, the brothers operated with a sense of insurgent mission, waging war on behalf of the underserved customer, who in Yonghui's case was the Chinese mother. "Safe, fresh, good value food for the Chinese mother" is how the company's mission statement reads today. Xuansong explained it to us. "To deliver that mission," he said, "demands that we focus most of our attention on the supply chain, and to source the highest-quality food from the most trusted suppliers. You would think this would be clear to all; what really matters the most and differentiates us ultimately is our supply chain. That is where we must be the most excellent." But this is not so easy to do, he continued, in a complex, fast-growing business, in a fast-growing country, and in an industry that is rapidly spawning new competitors and witnessing major shifts in channels and delivery modes due to the Internet and mobile digital technologies.

The secret to their success, the brothers told us, is that they have focused relentlessly on the essence of their insurgency as they've grown, and have paid special attention to what differentiates them. "When I was growing up in China," Xuansong said, "there was a great volleyball player who helped us win the medal in the 1984 Olympics. Her name was Lang Ping and she was called the Iron Hammer. She was known for her spike; if you could set her up well, she would win the point. In our business, a major role my brother and I play is to remind people that our supply chain is like Lang Ping. We win if we spike it. We have become convinced that this focus and awareness is *the* thing that matters more than anything else we can do as leaders and founders. Leaders must keep things simple and focused, especially in the turbulent and distracting environment in which we now compete."

So far, it's working. The Yonghui fresh-produce core was so successful that it now accounts for around 40 percent of the store's economics, compared to less than 20 percent for its rivals. Over the past five years, Yonghui has grown at a 32 percent annual rate.

The company now operates more than three hundred stores and takes in $5 billion in profitable revenues.

The most powerful insurgencies have several mutually reinforcing attributes. One is a *bold mission*, of the sort that has fueled the phenomenal growth of Yonghui. Another is *spikiness*: a constant emphasis on what differentiates the company and makes it unique. Yet another, the idea of a *limitless horizon*: the idea that a company, if massively successful, can intelligently extend the boundaries of its core further and further outward. You see this especially come into play in the stories of companies that have maintained their insurgent focus and energy even at large scale—companies such as IKEA and Apple.

A sharp insurgent mission should provide a company with its focus and purpose, both inside and outside. It is at its most powerful when pushed down into personnel systems, advertising, product features, and customer focus in a way that makes it real and forces trade-offs that shape the company, by helping determine who to hire and promote, which suppliers to choose, and what investments to make. Great statements of insurgency jump right out at the people they are supposed to reach. Google's objective—"Organize all of the world's information"—grabs you right away with its ambitious simplicity. CavinKare, an Indian consumer-products company that has enjoyed an almost eightfold increase in revenues since 2000, has built itself and its product offerings around this core idea: "Whatever a rich man enjoys, the common man should be able to afford." IKEA is an especially good example of the lasting power of a great insurgent mission. Founded in 1943 and still family owned, the company is now into the third generation of ownership and has grown to 150,000 employees, yet it has barely strayed from its original mission, originally articulated in a document titled "Testament of a Furniture Dealer." That mission—"to offer a wide range of well-designed, functional home furnishing products at prices so low that as many people as possible will be able to afford them"—is nothing less than the company's soul, as every great mission should be. The lesson is simple: stay true to your mission in everything you do, no matter what your size, and you're more likely to succeed. Lose touch with it, and you're more likely to fail.

Front-Line Obsession

Most founders were their company's first salesperson, its first product developer, or both. They lived and breathed the front line, driven by an intellectual curiosity about every detail of the customer experience and of how everything in the business works. They used instincts formed at the ground level to make every decision.

An obsession with the front line is fundamental to the founder's mentality. It shows up in three ways—as an obsession with front-line employees, with individual customers at all levels of the company, and with the details of the business. This is the mentality that Wexner has brought to L Brands, and it's the mentality that the young M. S. Oberoi, who grew up poor in what is now Pakistan, brought to the Oberoi Group, one of the world's great luxury-hotel companies. Oberoi began his career as a penniless hotel clerk in rural India, learning the business absolutely from the bottom up. He founded the hotel chain in 1934 on a shoestring. Three years later he raised the money to buy the Grand Hotel in Calcutta, which he was able to acquire because its price had hit rock bottom after a cholera epidemic. That's the kind of classically courageous move that young insurgents make. During World War II, to finance his purchase, Oberoi resourcefully turned the hotel into a barracks for British soldiers.

Oberoi obsessed about every detail that might affect the customer experience in his hotels: the length of bellmen's trousers, the temperature of the tea, the freshness of the flowers, the placement of signage. Even in his eighties, he was still visiting his hotels to make sure employees were getting everything right. In doing so, he established a culture by which all employees shared in his obsession, which is why, more than a decade after his death, Oberoi hotels are still some of the world's most successful. In 2015, *Travel & Leisure* named Oberoi the best hotel brand in the world, and its hotel in Udaipur, India, as the best hotel in the world. The founder's mentality lives on.

The front-line obsession is the essence of Oberoi's competitive advantage, and the company maintains it by ensuring that all aspects of staffing—from hiring to training to promotion—track back to attention to customer detail. At any Oberoi hotel, the employees on the front line are individually responsible and empowered to directly create value for the customer. During an average stay, an Oberoi customer will come into contact forty-two separate times with staff members, each of whom has the discretion to make decisions as he or she sees fit, even at the level, say, of giving a scarf to a customer on the way to visit a sick friend. To maintain a personal connection with each customer, the staff members meet nightly to go over the next day's arrival list and to review each new guest's history and preferences. Employees get special training on emotional intelligence, with two aims: listening with empathy and understanding each guest's unique needs. Even the most senior managers are encouraged to be humble and to model behaviors, by checking in guests when necessary, by clearing tables at busy times, or even by moving bags. Every month, groups of employees meet in an organized way to share experiences and capture best practices. In one of the hotel kitchens we visited, we saw a sign above the vegetable-washing table that read "Improve Everything You Touch."

The hotel tries to segment customers in a way that they can anticipate special needs. Poornima Bhambal, an assistant manager at The Oberoi Udaivilas, Udaipur, described how the hotel builds systems to look for patterns of past stays and cultural indicators, so that the staff members can anticipate needs that customers may not yet even have. For instance, they know that some types of guests always ask for special dental or shaving kits and put them in the room. Other guests expect twenty-four-hour child care, so the hotel simply offers it at check-in. Guests with very long trips to the hotel have a special fast track that gets them to their room within two minutes of arrival. As Bhambal said, describing their methods for anticipating needs, "Unless you put yourself in a guest's shoes, you will never know." The attention to detail and front-line empowerment, parts of a finely honed and highly data-driven guest-management system, are the core of the Oberoi's competitive advantage in an industry where customer service standards are constantly rising. Oberoi has succeeded for decades by leading the way, not following.

Today, the CEO of the group that controls the Oberoi and Trident Hotel chains is Vikram Oberoi, a grandson of M. S. Oberoi. When we met, he told us about visiting his grandfather when he was in his nineties. "My grandfather's sight declined with age," he said, "and he had to resort to very thick glasses and would have to hold reading materials about four inches away. But I remember, time after time, visiting him at his house and finding him holding guest surveys up to his nose and constantly making notes to send to the hotel managers about his observations. He remained obsessed with the smallest detail about how the hotels were serving our guests right up until the end. He was the ultimate role model."

Another critical element of the front-line obsession is deep curiosity about how the business is working in its details at the front line. M. S. Oberoi demonstrated this by attending to every last detail in his hotels around the world. He insisted that his chefs visit food markets themselves, rather than ordering food to be delivered unseen. He discussed plumbing problems with his managers. He lasered in on the right detail at the right time. His son, P. R. S. Oberoi, now the chairman of the group that runs the business, has carried on this tradition. He has been known to randomly check even eggs in the kitchen, cracking them and inspecting their color. But M. S. Oberoi did not let his belief in the importance of attention to detail slow anything down. He had a reputation for clearing his desk of every file before leaving every day. Without a haystack, he felt, you can't lose any needles.

In the high-touch consumer business of luxury hotels, an obsession with the front line is the essence of competitive differentiation. However, you can find the same trait in all sorts of great founder-mentality companies, across a wide range of industries. These are often the most lasting performers. Think of Steve Jobs at Apple, and how much he focused on the simple elegance of the motherboard design inside his products, even though the customer would not see it. Or think of how obsessively Toyota focuses on the front-line jobs in its factory production system, where all operators have the right, indeed the obligation, to shut down the line and trigger a problem-solving effort if they see any kind of production problem in front of them. The most enduring companies in fast-changing industries manage to maintain their front-line obsession and love of detail even as they grow large.

The Owner's Mindset

Small companies possess one great competitive advantage over incumbents. At every level of the business, the employees of small companies make their decisions and pursue their objectives motivated by an owner's mindset. They're so invested in the company, that is, that they feel and act like owners, something that can't be said of the layers of staff and professional managers at large incumbents. As we noted in the introduction, surveys show that only 13 percent of employees feel any emotional connection or engagement with the company at which he or she works.[1] That's a startling number, and it represents an opportunity for companies to inspire their employees with an owner's mindset. The difference between employees who operate with the owner's mindset and those who don't can be as great as the difference between devoted parents and restless babysitters.

Three ingredients make up the essence of the owner's mindset and establish it as a source of competitive advantage. The first is a *strong cost focus*—treating both expenses and investments as though they are your own money. The second advantage is what we call a *bias to action*. Adi Godrej, who runs Godrej Group, a leading Indian consumer-goods company, exhibits this bias in how he runs its operations. "It is our superior speed to make big decisions and take actions on them," he told us, "that lets us constantly outmaneuver larger global consumer-goods companies that come into our markets." The third advantage is an *aversion to bureaucracy*—an aversion, that is, to the layers of organization, headquarters departments, and hordes of corporate staff that can accumulate, capture power, and create complex decision processes that clog the arteries of a business and slow it down.

Many companies lose the competitive edge of the owner's mindset as they grow. That's because they become complex, turn into public companies with diffuse ownership, hire professional managers with short tenures (the average public-company CEO lasts only about five years), build up enormous corporate staffs, and experience a balkanization of budgets that traps resources inside of departments with their own agendas, making them hard to find and to redeploy. Again, this creates an opportunity: those companies that can grow large while still maintaining some of the speed, efficiency, and focus of a young founder-led company have an enormous competitive advantage and, our research shows, are the big winners when it comes to value creation.

Take AB InBev, the largest and most profitable beer company in the world, with revenues of $50 billion, a market value of $186 billion, and a profit margin of 39 percent, more than ten points above the average of its largest rivals. Not many people would have bet on AB InBev at its start, but the company has succeeded beyond expectations by assiduously cultivating the owner's mindset as it has grown.

The story begins in 1989, when three Brazilian private equity investors—Jorge Paulo Lemann, Marcel Telles, and Carlos Alberto Sicupira—purchased a marginally profitable local brewer called Brahma. They knew from looking around the world that a strong local beer business could be a huge money maker, and they set out with the objective of making their new brewery the most efficient in the world. To that end, they hired an expert in the Toyota Production System and launched an effort to benchmark and capture the practices of the lowest-cost global brewers. "From 1989 to 1999," Telles told us, "it was primarily an operational improvement story, and a story of creating a new culture with young, hungry talent, mostly from outside of the beer industry. The competitive culture we created essentially wore down Antarctica, our Brazilian competitor, who eventually had to merge with us, giving us strong leadership of the market."

Their plan succeeded well. Within just a few years, the company reapplied its cost systems and cultural practices in breweries from Bolivia to Paraguay and created the largest and most profitable beer company in South America. When we visited Telles in his office in the humble outskirts of São Paulo, on a hill overlooking a favela, or slum, he described the types of practices that the young company was using to reinforce an owner's mindset. There were no offices, even for the CEO, because the leadership team believed that closed offices led to a culture of hiding and of hierarchy. Targets for every group, all the way to the CEO, were projected onto a big screen in the main office area, with the targets color-coded according to their status. Everyone could see how others were doing, and how each piece connected to the whole. Hiring focused heavily on young people with a hunger to succeed. Budgets were looked at from the ground up each year, and *every* cost mattered.

Today, the company has become a global powerhouse that has captured nearly one-fourth of the world's beer market. It merged with Interbrew in Europe, acquired Anheuser-Busch in America, and acquired Modelo in Mexico, along with a host of local brands and breweries. The company even launched a bid for SABMiller in 2015. In consolidating the global beer industry, it has constantly refined its practices and culture, embedding them into each new business acquired on the way, without ever changing its core repeatable model. The company works hard to instill the owner's mindset in all of its employees. "We are a company of owners," the company's statement of principles reads. "Owners take results personally."

One manager we met during our visit memorably summed up the company's approach. "We create restaurant owners, not waiters," he said. "If you're a restaurant owner, and a new restaurant opens across the street serving the same food, how do you feel? You feel like someone is putting your livelihood at risk, threatening you, threatening your family. It's personal, because the restaurant is your dream. But if you are a waiter, and a new restaurant opens across the street, how do you feel? At best, indifferent. Actually, there's now competition for your services. Many companies inadvertently create waiters. We work tirelessly to create restaurant owners."

But its founders have not stopped with beer. Their private investment firm, 3G Capital, recently purchased Kraft and Heinz, and intends to rebuild those companies using the same principles and owner's mindset that worked so well for them at AB InBev.

For more than twenty years, we've encouraged clients to "think like an owner"—to review their strategies with an owner's mindset, which means aligning the broad interests of the company's leaders and shareholders. The power of this approach has been central to the rise of the private equity industry. We see it as a reaction against the bureaucracy, poor cost management, and complexity that beset many large companies as they drift away from the founder's mentality. When we analyzed the returns of a range of different types of deals within several private equity funds that we know well, we found that of all deal types, the ones that earned nearly 50 percent more than the others were businesses sold by large, public companies in which the management had seemingly lost the owner's mindset and the incentives of ownership. When private equity firms restored the owner's mindset at these companies, this consistently increased speed, reduced bureaucracy, caused a more critical evaluation of noncore businesses, and improved the management of costs. The consistency with which a return to the owner's mindset propelled high returns to private equity firms is one of the most profound phenomena of the past few decades in business. In the interviews we've conducted with founders and founding families around the world, we've heard the same thing—that the owner's mindset has provided them with a consistent source of competitive advantage.

For the past couple of decades, many of us have talked about the owner's mindset as *the* best way for companies to succeed. But we've come to realize that there's more to the story than that. The owner's mindset is only part of the story. That's why we've made it just one of the three defining traits of the founder's mentality, which, we believe, represents a significantly more powerful way for companies big and small to achieve sustained profitable growth. The owner's mindset aligns the interests of leaders and shareholders, but the founder's mentality goes beyond that and also aligns the interests of leaders and the employees who work at the front line, where a business meets its customers. It demands innovation and is profoundly customer-centric: a posture that, we believe, ultimately creates the most value.

In the owner mindset discussions of the late 1980s and early 1990s, people very rarely talked about the front line. The focus on aligning the interests of leaders and shareholders at times led to an incumbent mindset: a concern with hunkering down and extracting value from the existing business, and a loss of the impulse to innovate, serve customers uniquely, and fully value the employees on the front line. That's a major impediment to sustainable growth, one that, as we'll explain in this book, the founder's mentality can help you avoid.

Learning How to Infuse the Founder's Mentality in Your Organization

Though all of our examples so far have been founder-led companies, we should note here that many founders do *not* exhibit the founder's mentality. All founders are different, of course, and many succeed or run their companies into the ground because of the unique strengths and weaknesses of their personalities. Our focus in this book will be on a mentality, not a personality—a collection of specific behaviors and attitudes, best exemplified by the traits of great founders, that if properly cultivated in the rest of the organization can lead more reliably to sustainable growth.

It doesn't matter if your company is decades removed from the era of its founding. Our point is that just about every company, at any stage in its life, can benefit from the attitudes and behaviors that make up the founder's mentality. Young companies need to *build* the founder's mentality; older companies need to *rediscover* or even *redefine* it. This book will show how.

What the Data Shows

We've explored the three traits of the founder's mentality at length by surveying executives and examining databases of companies and their behaviors, and we've found that 90 percent of the time, leaders cite at least one of these traits as a source of the founder's advantage.[2] Our work with this data has also made clear to us that the founder's mentality can provide benefits not just to young or small companies. Companies of all ages and sizes that were able to maintain the founder's mentality are more likely to be top performers. In fact, companies able to attain a reasonable level of scale and market power while maintaining the founder's mentality prove to be the best-performing companies in the world. The best fifth of performers in our own database, for example, had high insurgency characteristics 74 percent of the time, versus 19 percent for the poorest-performing fifth. For front-line obsession, the difference was nearly a factor of five—57 percent versus 12 percent. For the owner's mindset, the difference was about the same—50 percent versus 9 percent (see figure 1-2).[3]

On the surface, the three traits of the founder's mentality look like basic business. But they're surprisingly hard to retain as companies grow. Complexity sets in, rewarding the masters of internal politics and process; power shifts away from the front line to the center; bureaucracy takes over. Gradually, internally, companies lose the founder's mentality, and externally they start drifting off course, onto the path toward failure.

How does your company rate on the traits of the founder's mentality? Take the brief survey in the sidebar to find out.

FIGURE 1-2

Top performers adhere to the traits of founder's mentality

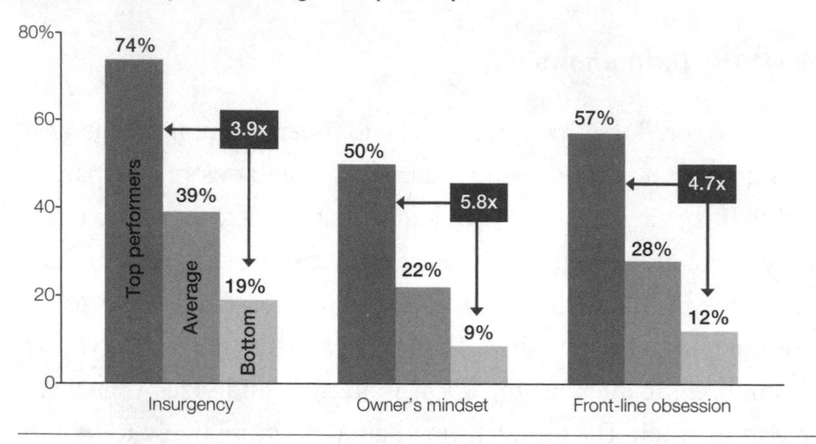

Does Your Organization Have a Founder's Mentality?

A company has the founder's mentality when its employees live and breathe the principles and entrepreneurial approach characteristic of great founders. The Founder's Mentality® diagnostic survey is the first step in the process of understanding whether your company is really retaining the founder's mentality as it grows, and the biggest internal barriers that are eroding it. For a more detailed version that shows respondents how they rate on the individual attributes of the founder's mentality, you can take the survey online on our website at www.foundersmentality.com. To get started, consider each of the following statements and rate yourself or your organization using a numerical scale where 1 = "Strongly Disagree" and 5 = "Strongly Agree."

The Founder's Mentality

Insurgency		
Bold mission	• We are clear about the "big why"—the unique purpose for why we are in business.	_
	• I find our mission to be personally energizing and inspiring to those around me.	_
"Spikiness"	• Our organization is clear on the one or two capabilities that drive our differentiation with customers.	_
	• We have a repeatable model for growth that will allow us to capture or extend leadership in our markets.	_
Limitless horizons	• We are focused on the long term in our investments and our budgetary decisions; managing quarterly earnings is truly secondary.	_
	• We embrace turbulence and are experimenting and building new business models ahead of the competition.	_
Front-line obsession		
Relentless experimentation	• We innovate and experiment a lot in the field; this drives our learning and is a competitive advantage.	_
	• We have an efficient feedback process in place to help us understand what is working and take corrective action quickly.	_
Front-line empowerment	• We are the most sought-after employer by top talent in our industry.	_
	• We treat our front-line people as the heroes of our business and do whatever is needed to support them.	_
Customer advocacy	• We are clear about who our core customers are; their loyalty is a competitive advantage.	_
	• The voice of the customer is fully represented in all important meetings.	_
Owner's mindset		
Strong cash focus	• We have a sharp focus on cash and costs; we treat each dollar as if it is our own.	_
	• We rapidly redeploy people and capital wherever they are most critical to the business.	_
Bias for action	• Our organization makes and acts upon key decisions faster than our competitors; speed is an advantage for us.	_
	• People in the organization are quick to take on personal responsibility and risk to do the right thing.	_
Aversion to bureaucracy	• We have simplified our initiatives to focus on the biggest priorities that deliver value.	_
	• Our planning and review processes are the best in our industry, efficiently reallocating resources to make our front line more competitive.	_

(continued)

(continued)

Overall statements

- Our biggest barriers to growth and future success are much more internal than external; our fate is in our hands. _
- Our main competitors five years from now will be different companies than those in the past five years. _

Scoring

At the highest level is your cumulative score. The data we've seen typically groups companies in four ranges, from a strong founder's mentality (total score across all statements is greater than 75), to waning (total score of 60–75), to low (total score of 45–60), to founder's mentality lost (total score is less than 45).

While the overall score is a strong indicator of a company's health on the inside and its ability to sustain profitable growth on the outside, the pattern is even more important for identifying the highest level of issues. This is because companies don't lose the founder's mentality uniformly, but see big drops in one or another dimension.

Taking this further and ultimately drilling down to the root cause of decline is critical (that is, understanding the unresolved issues that the front line is grappling with, getting real feedback from customers, and so on). This book will illustrate how to do that.

The Founder's Mentality Map

By harnessing the power of all three of these traits, companies like L Brands have managed to scale and—even more difficult—sustain profitable growth over time. But few businesses make that journey successfully, and fewer remain there for decades. Most, buffeted by the predictable crises of growth, are gradually pushed away from the benefits of the founder's mentality and the benefits of scale, and instead drift off course in predictable ways. Before we start exploring them in detail, though, let's start by taking a schematic look at the terrain on which this all plays out.

Figure 1-3 is the general map that we will use to chart the predictable stages and crises of companies as they move through the business life cycle. The map has two dimensions. The east-west axis represents *the net benefits of the founder's mentality* (a measure of the internal strength of the company and its culture) and the north-south axis represents *the net benefits of size* (a measure of the external strength of a company relative to competitors in its industry, a product of market power and scale).

Companies in the bottom right, where most companies start their journeys, are what we refer to as *insurgents.* They are young and have attained relatively little scale, but are propelled by a big idea and the internal strengths of the founder's mentality: namely, a missionary zeal for changing the standards in their industry; an

FIGURE 1-3

The founder's mentality map

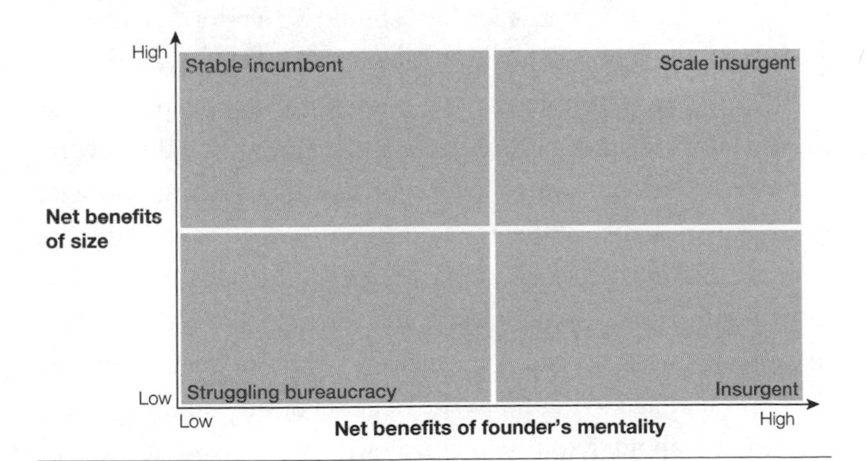

obsession with the people and the work done at the front line of the business; and the owner's mindset, a sense of deep personal responsibility for results that leads to a bias for speed and against bureaucracy.

Endeavor, a nonprofit organization dedicated to fostering the growth of young companies in developing economies, now has a network that extends to more than a thousand companies in more than twenty markets. These companies, with whom we spoke extensively during the course of our research, are exemplary insurgents. For instance, Alessandro Gardemann runs GEO Energética, a fifty-person Brazilian company that has a proprietary method to turn unused sugar-cane waste into energy—a process that has the potential to fill a large share of the demand for new energy in Brazil's rapidly growing economy. This company has the potential to scale to a large size, but with no shortage of practical challenges to go from insurgency to scale. It is an example of what we mean by a business that has made it through the start-up phase, has proven the power of its idea, and is now a young insurgent trying to achieve the benefits of scale.

In the upper right of our map in figure 1-3, you'll see what we believe most business leaders should strive for: *scale insurgency*. Scale insurgents are companies that have stayed true to their insurgency for a long time, have built market power and influence in the process, and retain the human vitality of the founder's mentality. AB InBev, Enterprise Rent-A-Car, Google, Haier, Apple, Victoria's Secret, and IKEA have all achieved scale insurgency. Ultimately, all of the advice in this book is designed to help companies achieve scale insurgency. Here, companies have grown to scale and achieved a position of leadership, yet they also manage to maintain the benefits of the founder's mentality. Only about 7 to 8 percent of all companies that grew to

$500 million (only about one start-up in two thousand makes it to that size at all) reached the position of *scale insurgency* over the past decade, but on average those few that did accounted for much more than half of the net value created in the global stock market each year.[4]

Incumbency, the position in the upper left of our map, is quite different. Companies here have largely lost the entrepreneurial energy and flexibility of the founder's mentality, yet they have attained a position of sustained strength, and perhaps even industry leadership, because of the assets and capabilities that they possess. They have created barriers to competition that serve as imposing defense fortifications, and they tend to be the largest companies. Well-known examples in this position include Microsoft, Gazprom, Unilever, and SAP.

The worst place to be on our map is the lower left: the realm of struggling bureaucracy. Companies in this position long ago lost the internal strengths of the founder's mentality, but they've either lost or never developed those defensive fortifications that protect successful incumbents. Most of the companies that end up here never recover their momentum. At the extreme, these are companies in which the scourge of complexity has disabled the ability to react rapidly to change, has slowed down the rate of learning to a crawl, and has driven up costs. Familiar examples include General Motors, Kodak, Sony, and Kmart. Though rapid, external events triggered the traumatic decline of each of these companies, their poor state of inner health made them especially vulnerable to the trauma and determined their fate.

Many companies don't exist at the extremes but instead drift toward the middle of the matrix—an inherently unstable position characterized by waning market power, internal dysfunction born of complexity and bureaucracy, and a sluggishness that impedes quick decision making. On balance, as these companies drift downward, they do not earn their cost of capital, and they therefore destroy value in the stock market.

The Journey North: Achieving Profitable Growth at Scale

As we'll show in the chapters ahead, success along both dimensions of our map leads to sustainable growth. We call this process *the journey north*: a journey from the realm of *start-up insurgency*, at the bottom right of our map, to the realm of *scale insurgency*, at the top right (see figure 1-4). This is the journey that Wexner has made successfully with L Brands, but it's a hard one to make without encountering trouble along one axis or the other. Success on one but not the other leads to instability for all but a handful of businesses. Failure on both leads to decline and eventual demise.

FIGURE 1-4

The journey north: Achieving profitable growth at scale

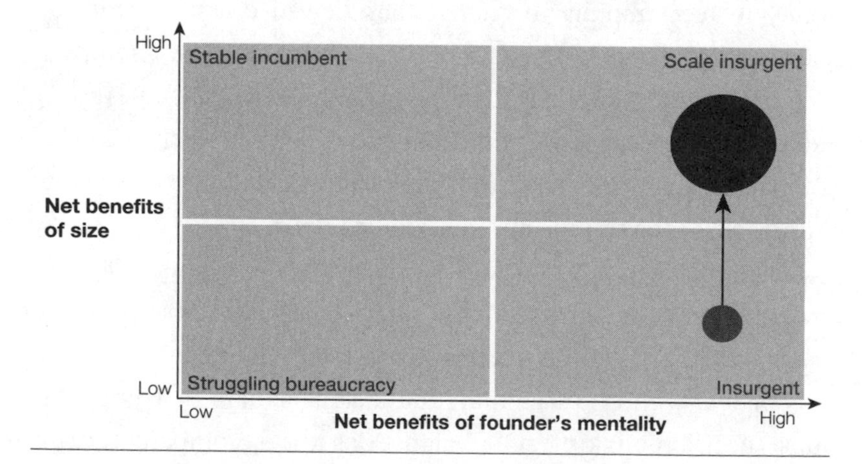

The Default Path: Problems That Come with Scale

Time and again in our research and our practice, we've observed companies following a default path on our map (see figure 1-5). It begins in the lower-right corner of the map. The company here is endowed with the positive traits of the founder's mentality and is often still founder-led, but it has little else but an idea and an enthusiastic team to work with. It needs to reach critical mass to compete; it needs to garner market power to create profitability; and it needs to do both at once to earn returns for investors and opportunities for employees. From there, the growing company moves north on our map, gaining in size and market power, yet often adding systems and complexity that dilute the internal energy of the founder's mentality.

This is where the *paradox of growth* comes into play. The internal strength and vitality of young companies, which allowed them to take on larger incumbents in the first place, often decline as those companies grow and succeed, adding process and structure, which

FIGURE 1-5

The default path: Problems that come with scale

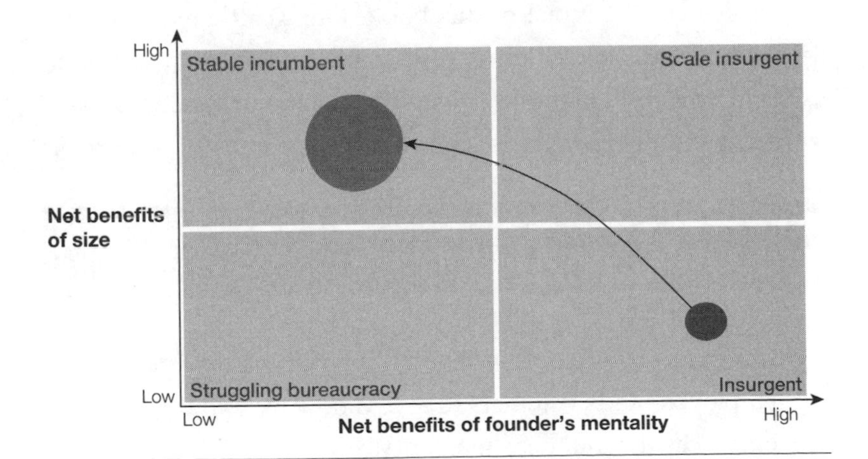

detract from the personal intimacy of the earlier founder years. As we will show, the problems that emerge in growing companies often trace directly to internal changes that erode the founder's mentality. That is why 85 percent of executives perceive that the key barriers to sustained and profitable growth that they face are on the inside.[5] Most observers don't recognize the extent of this problem, however, because nearly all measures of success—in a company's own reporting or in the analysis of those who follow it—track *external* results in the form of financial returns, growth rates, market share, and sometimes customer advocacy. These are critical, of course. But nobody would value a racehorse based solely on its past wins. To make sure its performance is sustainable, you also need to gauge its inner health—very carefully.

Three of the four quadrants on our map—*insurgency*, *incumbency*, and *struggling bureaucracy*—represent the terrain on which the predictable crises of growth play out. In the next chapter, we'll take a look at these crises and how they arise.

A quick note, however, before we do. In the chapters ahead, we will *not* be outlining a program for how businesses can engineer lasting cultural change within themselves. That's a process that requires years of sustained effort on the part of leadership teams, and it's beyond the scope of this book. Our goal here is to identify practical ideas for achieving sustainable growth that can lead to results in a much shorter time frame than the five to seven years that experts on culture estimate is required for deep cultural change.

USING THE FOUNDER'S MENTALITY IN YOUR ORGANIZATION

✓ Using the survey in this chapter, interview front-line employees and customers to assess how well your company embraces the founder's mentality.

✓ Armed with interview results, start one-on-one discussions with your top managers, asking:

- Does everyone understand the company's insurgent mission?
- Are we focused on empowering/supporting the front line?
- Do we think and act like owners?
- Do we share the ambition to become the scale insurgent in our industry?
- Can we learn from competitors, especially newly emerging insurgents, who embody the founder's mentality better?
- How do answers to these questions change our business priorities?

2

The Three Predictable Crises of Growth

How Great Companies Lose Their Way

In most of this book, we will present practical approaches to anticipating and addressing the crises of growth, many originating in the practices of great founders. But before we turn to the solutions, we need to describe the problems. So let's turn to them now.

Overload: The Crisis of High Growth

To grow a company from $100 million to $1 billion, or from $500 million to $5 billion, you have to change how you work. You can't just do the same things you've always done, only ten times more often. You have to build new systems to handle escalating complexity, and you have to adapt your business to the marketplace. Once, you could do everything you needed to with an Excel spreadsheet personally designed by your CFO; now you've got an SAP installation in its place, manned by a department of IT specialists. Once, by force of will alone, your founding team, surrounded by an inexperienced staff, could carry the day; now your company's size and rate of growth demand that you hire a different level of talent, from companies whose culture is not like your own. Once, your founding team knew everything at all times and could make its decisions in one place; now you need to push decisions down through the organization in consistent ways. Once, you yourself could be everywhere to model behaviors; now you simply can't. Once, you knew your key customers by their first names; now you know them as averages on PowerPoint slides. Once, everyone in your company knew what made your mission special; now you have trouble conveying that sense to the outer reaches of the organization.

Overload hits when a company is scaling up aggressively—when it is moving up from the bottom-right quadrant of our founder's mentality map, that is, and aiming to reach to the upper-right quadrant.

As companies scale, their leaders tend to undermanage or take the elements of the founder's mentality for granted. This is natural, but the result is that they start to lose what made them great in the first place. Complexity, systems, and processes slow them down, soak up more of their profitability, and blur their original sense of purpose. Overload afflicts growing companies that have failed to prepare adequately on the inside for the strains of size and complexity. It feels horrible: you're growing successfully and are working harder than ever, but with each passing day you feel more and more overwhelmed. You suffer from the sense that something dark is about to take hold.

Let's turn to the example of Norwegian Cruise Line. Once the leader in the cruise industry, the company was innovative and had strong growth ambitions and aggressive investors. Nonetheless, it ran aground. Why? Because it couldn't cope with overload. It hadn't properly developed systems to implement its growth strategy internally, and so that strategy broke down at dozens of points of execution on the front line—with customers, crew, staff on the shore, and the company's travel agent partners.

In what follows, we'll describe how Norwegian got into trouble on the journey north, and then we'll revisit the story in chapter 3, where we'll discuss how new leaders stepped in and used the founder's mentality to rebuild the business from the bottom up. The ultimate results were impressive: since that rebuilding effort, sales have nearly doubled, operating income has increased more than twelvefold, and growth has increased from zero to more than twenty percent.

Norwegian Cruise Line: Heavy Sailing

Norwegian Cruise Line launched today's modern cruise industry. Its founders, Knut Kloster and Ted Arison, put their first vessel in the water in 1966: a cruise ship designed to carry cars and offer low-cost voyages from Miami to the Caribbean. Norwegian was an innovator in its field, the first company to offer round-trip cruises that nearly anybody could afford. Under Kloster's leadership (Arison left to found Carnival Cruise Line), the company soon became a market leader, but then gradually fell behind its competitors. By the late 1990s, it had made a series of acquisitions and divestitures and taken in other investors, and overload hit. Struggling financially, with over $100 million in negative cash flow, the company agreed to be acquired in 2000 by Star Cruises, a leading cruise operator in Asia.

After the acquisition, Star Cruises announced aggressive plans to transform the company. Its first giant step was to introduce a break in the traditional cruise product by offering guests what it called Freestyle Cruising, which provided multiple dining and entertainment venues with flexible times, as opposed to the industry model at the time of single venues with set times. Ships not designed to handle this concept were dry-docked and retrofitted. The concept was revolutionary in the industry, but the execution proved difficult, especially for dining. Galleys were separated from dining areas, resulting in passengers waiting a long time for food. Guests grew exasperated, and the crew, feeling battered by dissatisfied guests and the stress of rolling out this new offering, grew upset and disengaged. But the company pushed ahead aggressively on expansion nonetheless, growing for the sake of growth, driving down prices through poor pricing discipline, and wreaking havoc on guest satisfaction and employee engagement. The bottom line? The company lost the trust of its front-line employees, the commitment of its travel agent partners, and the loyalty of its passengers, who increasingly switched to other vacation sources.

By 2007, having been unable to cope with overload, even under its new ownership, Norwegian had fallen seriously behind in its growth aspirations and profit plan. That's when its board (and the new owner, Apollo Investment Corporation) appointed Kevin Sheehan, a veteran executive with experience in the car-rental and entertainment industries, first as CFO and later as CEO.

Sheehan, who in his youth had driven taxis in Queens, New York, was known as a leader with a practical sense of how businesses work at the front line. He and his team immediately saw what Norwegian needed—"a transformation from the ground up," he told us, "starting with the front-line employees and our on-board customers." He saw that Norwegian's leaders had devoted too much of their time and attention to ideas generated in headquarters without sufficiently detailed front-line testing, follow-up, or practical embedding into the routines of the company.

We met with Sheehan on board *Norwegian Star*, one of his company's ships, where he described to us the situation he encountered when he took over as CEO. "When I joined," he said, "I spent a lot of time talking to front-line employees on ship and at the ports. I quickly realized that our biggest problems were internal, not related to the industry. We had pioneered Freestyle Cruising, but we were executing poorly, resulting in long lines and unhappy passengers. We were pricing in a uniform way, yet the truth is that there was a huge difference in value across cabins, and we needed a sophisticated yield system, like we had in the rental-car business, to match demand and value and pricing dynamically. Our travel agent partners were frustrated with us for last-minute price discounting and did not feel like real partners. And most importantly, our front-line employees had lost a sense of what was important. Were we a price cutter? An innovator? Customer-focused? What?"

This is a classic example of the breakdowns of overload. Norwegian was in a growing industry, in a leading position, with good ideas (like freestyle) about how the company would be differentiated and special. But as it grew, the company failed on several fronts. It failed to translate its strategy into front-line understanding. It failed to design systems to manage its more complex customer experience smoothly. It failed to involve the front line in the development of scheduling software for passengers and failed to connect the front line to the travel agent partners who were selling berths on the ships.

Chaos ensued inside the company. Unable to sell its new offering, and feeling it had no other option, it adopted a low-cost strategy on the outside, in the form of last-minute price cutting. And that strategy only made things worse. As the pressures of overload increased—a process compounded by the changes in ownership, which put more and more distance between management and the front line—Norwegian rapidly lost touch with the founder's mentality. Sheehan recognized that when he took over the company. In the next chapter, we'll explore how this insight helped him turn the company around and make it a successful scale insurgent.

Stall-Out: The Crisis of Low or Slowing Growth

Stall-out hits companies that have successfully scaled and are now struggling with the challenges of complexity. Rising levels of bureaucracy and internal dysfunction threaten to overwhelm the engines that powered them to success. Stall-out afflicts incumbents, which occupy the upper-left quadrant on our founder's mentality map. It's a disorienting crisis: leaders know their company is losing momentum, but when they pull the levers that have allowed them in the past to speed up or change direction, they get little response. They know *something* is different, but the complexity of their organization makes it hard for them to figure out what's different or what to do about it.

Stall-out is a predictable but dangerous crisis. Consider the following:

It's common. At Bain & Company, we track the performance of more than eight thousand global companies, and when we look at the data, here's what we see: of the roughly one in five companies that managed to make it through insurgency to incumbency in a recent fifteen-year period, two-thirds faced stall-out.[1] That includes such notables as Panasonic, Sony, Time Warner, Sharp, Bristol-Myers Squibb, Philips, and Mazda. Moreover, of the large companies that hit stall-out, fewer than one in seven will recover its market power and prior momentum.

It can happen fast. We recently studied fifty large companies in stall-out, tracing their growth rate in revenues through time, and what we discovered was stunning. These companies stalled out surprisingly suddenly, losing their growth momentum in only a few years and then turning rapidly downward, with rates that often dropped from double digits to low single digits or even negative numbers (see figure 2-1). This mirrors the findings of an extensive earlier study by the Corporate Executive Board, which examined fifty years of stall-out in American public companies. "Growth does not descend gradually," the authors of that study concluded, "it drops like a stone."[2]

It's an internal problem, caused by growth. Ninety-four percent of large-company executives cite internal dysfunction as their key barrier to continued profitable growth.[3] The irony, of course, is that this dysfunction derives from the very things that young insurgents work so hard to achieve: size, recognition, experience, capabilities, capital, and market position. This isn't really a surprise. As companies grow in size and complexity, they lose the dexterity and the flexibility they need to sustain growth, which calls to mind what a seventy-year-old yoga teacher once told one of us about the human aging process. "You don't get old and get stiff," he said. "You get stiff and *then* you get old."

FIGURE 2-1

Speed of major stall-outs

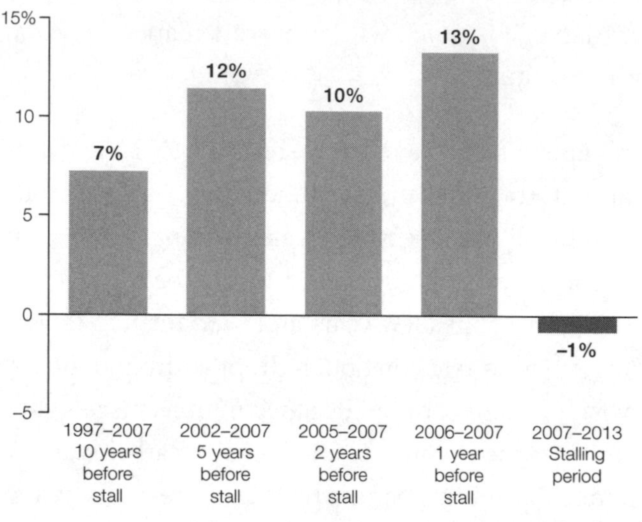

The Home Depot

Few stories illustrate the force of a stall-out better than what happened at The Home Depot, the largest home-improvement retailer in the world and the fourth-largest retailer in the United States.

The secret to The Home Depot's initial success traced to its remarkable founders, Bernard Marcus and Arthur Blank, who devoted themselves to building a company that would establish a close and direct advisory relationship with customers—a classic example of the founder's mentality in action. Their corporate mantra: "Whatever it takes." The two would personally tutor store employees in customer service. Employees, in turn, would offer clinics to shoppers on home-improvement projects and were always available in stores to offer knowledgeable advice.

The strategy set the company apart and generated powerful customer loyalty, and for years the company was a major success story. From the time of its founding in 1978 until 2000, The Home Depot consistently beat analyst expectations and eclipsed its 20 percent annual earnings growth targets. However, in December 2000, after missing an earnings target and being increasingly concerned about antiquated systems, especially IT, in a company that was approaching $50 billion in revenues, the board of directors brought on Robert Nardelli, a senior executive from GE, as CEO, to apply some big-company discipline.

Nardelli created a command-and-control environment. By early 2006, 98 percent of The Home Depot's top 170 executives were new to their jobs, and 56 percent of the new managers at headquarters had been brought in from the outside. Instead of continuing to make customer relationships and front-line enthusiasm the company's top priorities, as its founders had for so long, Nardelli and his team made cuts in those areas to boost quarterly profits, according to analysts. They replaced many long-serving full-time employees with lower-paid part-time workers, and customer service levels collapsed. "Do It Yourself," some people joked, now became "Find It Yourself." The bonds of trust among customers, store associates, and management were breached, eroding the founder's mentality.

When the University of Michigan released its annual American Customer Satisfaction Index in 2006, The Home Depot had slipped to dead last among major US retailers, with a score of sixty-seven, eleven points behind its main competitor, Lowe's, and three lower than even the much-maligned Kmart. From 2000 to 2007, the company's market value declined by 55 percent, and its stores had experienced their fourth year in a row of declining foot traffic and loss of position to its competitors.

To take a reading on the business, the board of directors held meetings in the field to hear from front-line employees, and they soon recognized a consistent pattern in what they heard. Worried about the future, employees repeatedly brought up the same subjects, which one board member described to us as "disempowerment of longtime store employees, and a feeling that the social contract between the company, its employees, and the customers was being breached."

We asked Greg Brenneman—a global turnaround expert who is also the company's longest-standing board member—to tell us more. "You could see the serious trouble bubbling up under the surface as you probed in the company," he said. "Though sales were increasing, foot traffic, the lifeblood of any retailer, had been going steadily down. Store managers were feeling shackled by dozens of financial templates and metrics that took time away from customers and running the stores. The most experienced store employees, the real experts on plumbing or electricity, had been let go and replaced with less experienced and cheaper part-time store workers. New stores, dialed up in their construction to push up growth and quarterly earnings, were not generating good returns, leading to further staff cuts. We were stalling out and needed to pursue a different course."

Indeed it did. Fortunately, the company replaced Nardelli with a new CEO, Frank Blake, who, tapping into the power of the founder's mentality, launched a series of initiatives focused on renewing bonds with front-line employees and the customer, and on running the stores well. In chapter 4, we'll examine in depth how the company turned itself around.

Free Fall: The Crisis of Obsolescence and Decline

Free fall can happen at any point in a company's life cycle. But it is most common in maturing incumbents whose business model has come under severe attack by new insurgents (think of bookstores attacked by Amazon) or is no longer as viable in a changing market (think of Blockbuster Video renting tapes in stores when the ability to download content began).

If you are one of the few ever to have lived through free fall, you know how terrible it feels. The loss of momentum and control. The anxiety as you feel your company tipping into a nosedive. The downward spiral of events. The prospect of onrushing catastrophe. The realization that the levers that used to work so well no longer seem to work at all.

In stall-out, which was bad enough, you had time to ponder your next move, and you probably had lots of options. In free fall, though, you're hurtling toward a crash and you're running out of time.

Of the three predictable crises of growth, free fall is the most treacherous. At any given moment today, about 5 to 7 percent of companies are either in free fall or about to tip into it. And here's a sobering fact: only about 10 to 15 percent of those companies, depending on your definition of success, ever pull out of it. Moreover, half of those that manage this feat do so only by fundamentally redefining at least a part of their core business.[4] The time is past for these companies to *rediscover* the insurgency. Quickly—very quickly—they have to *redefine* it.

At first, the causes of free fall usually appear to be external: a global financial crisis, a banking-system collapse, government deregulation, or, more commonly, a new business model or technology, harnessed by a nimble insurgent competitor. These forms of market turbulence are the visible face of the problem, and they're on the rise. We estimate that in the decade from 1985 to 1994, only about half of markets were being buffeted by forces that we define as turbulent, whereas two decades later, from 2005 to 2014, close to two in three were.[5] But turbulence tends to be the *trigger* of free fall, not the cause. Usually, the root cause is internal, not external: the company did not prepare for the external problem, did not adapt fast enough, or did not have a second-generation engine for its business ready to go when the first-generation engine became obsolete.

The symptoms of free fall are extreme. Your financial performance worsens rapidly. Your growth prospects and your market value tumble. Analysts and investors begin to shriek. Important physical measures of your success, such as customer loyalty and market share, deteriorate in ways you have not seen before. Your family and friends start to worry about you. Think of Kodak, which in the 1990s was the apparently unassailable leader in its market, with 80 percent market share in its core film business, but which then went into a free fall that led to its bankruptcy in 2012. Since 2000, all sorts of other once-dominant companies have taken a similar plunge, among them AIG, Blockbuster, Gateway, General Motors, Lehman Brothers, Nintendo, Panasonic, RIM, and Sharp, just to name a few.

When we asked a Kodak executive who lived through the company's free fall to explain what happened, he gave us a simple answer: "Digital." That's the explanation you'll usually hear when Kodak's story comes up, and the sudden rise of digital technology is indeed an important factor in a growing number of cases of free fall. But to us, it's dangerously incomplete. The rise of digital technology precipitated an industry shift that triggered Kodak's descent into free fall, but what sealed the company's fate was that it wasn't prepared to weather a storm. And the reason for *that* was internal, not external.

To understand free fall a little better, let's take a look at the story of Charles Schwab, a company that began its life imbued with the spirit of the founder's mentality, became one of the best-performing stocks for over a decade, and then found itself in free fall, plummeting toward disaster.

Charles Schwab: Descent into Free Fall

The story begins in 1973, when Schwab, then a young investment adviser, decided to create a discount brokerage firm in San Francisco, California, that would cater to the small but competent investor. With the deregulation of brokerage commissions just two years away, he felt that he could create a unique firm that could reach do-it-yourself investors who wanted control over their accounts, valued simple tools of investing, and did not want to pay high commissions.

Schwab launched his company with a powerful and incredibly useful insurgent mission. "Chuck started the firm out of a deep sense of personal outrage that the brokerage industry systematically exploited its customers," John Kador writes in *Charles Schwab: How One Company Beat Wall Street and Reinvented the Brokerage Industry*.[6] Fueled by this founder-led sense of outrage, Schwab quickly became an innovation leader, offering its customers the first electronic investment tools, the first major mutual-fund supermarket (OneSource), the lowest rates in the industry, and the first online trading platform. In short, the company brought the Internet to the independent investor for the first time, and investors flocked to the company in the decades that followed. By the 1990s, the company's stock price had increased more than a hundredfold, and it had become the best-performing company of its type in financial services. "We were buying lunch for everyone, hiring fast, feeling the wind at our back," one executive told us about life at Schwab at the end of the 1990s. "Trades had doubled in the prior year alone, and we were bringing in people as fast as we could hire them."

But then, suddenly, three different external storms blew in at once. One involved the collapse of the Internet bubble and the decline in the market values of technology stocks—a huge component of Schwab's trading. Another involved the arrival of new insurgent competitors like E*Trade and Ameritrade, which emerged with super-low-cost business models that targeted Internet-empowered day traders and electronic traders, who had become a large part of the industry profit pool. And the third involved the decline in stock market volume caused by the outside market collapse. It was a triple whammy of disruption, and Schwab, it turned out, couldn't cope. "Our trading volume collapsed by 50 percent," the Schwab executive told us. "The people we had hired in such a frenzy were often not as good, degrading customer service. We began to see our customer scores falling. The decline in revenues and pricing compression due to new competitors revealed the extent we had let costs creep up. But the interpretation was very loose, and the solutions that were in the air at the time—some of which were to add even more customer services—were not going to restore order."

In 2000, worried about its future, the company made a risky move away from its core: buying U.S. Trust, a high-end, old-school portfolio management business. This was precisely the sort of company that Schwab had been founded to oppose. Schwab executives made the move for reasons of diversification and to provide a broader suite of services to customers, but it served only to erode its core, not renew it. One high-level executive at the time, Charles Goldman, remembers feeling deeply concerned. "The U.S. Trust acquisition added huge complexity just when we did not need it," he told us. "Suddenly, in the midst of crisis, we owned a bank on a different coast, with a different culture, with regulatory issues we did not understand. Huge management time was sucked into this, and it was a real distraction, given the burning platform in our core business."

At the same time, in another effort to save the company, the leadership team launched an initiative titled Project Renaissance, which created eight different customer segments with different offers and new services. The theory was that more sophisticated customer offerings would preserve pricing, but in practice they created what one executive described to us as "a nightmare of complexity that started to really confuse our message to the customer." The company then expanded further into the capital markets business and began branching out internationally. "We got sucked into one initiative after another that had the effect of pulling us farther from solving the real problem," Goldman said.

As its free fall accelerated, Schwab saw its internal dynamics worsen and began to realize that the difficulty in responding to the crisis outside had deep roots inside the company itself. "The culture shifted to avoiding downside," one executive told us. "People became more concerned with keeping their job than with doing it right. Senior executives were acting like agents rather than principals." Another manager recalled, "We found that we had created an impossible bureaucracy. The voices that were the loudest were the voices of the staff who reported to the CEO. These people dominated the meetings, while the line managers closer to the customers would sit there in frustration. It was like we had disenfranchised the people who really knew best what the problem was."

Mortifyingly for Charles Schwab himself, the low-cost upstart TD Waterhouse began running TV ads—featuring a crusty actor from the TV show *Law and Order*—that grouped Schwab along with Merrill Lynch and other traditional brokers: the big, complex, expensive companies that Schwab had always tried so hard to differentiate itself from. To make matters worse, the customer Net Promoter Score® (a measure of customer advocacy and loyalty)[7] in Schwab's retail business had declined to negative 34. The company now had 34 percent more detractors than supporters in its own customer base.

Investors noticed. From 2000 to early 2004, Schwab's market value dropped by about 75 percent. Aware of the need for an immediate and dramatic intervention, in 2004 the board of directors persuaded Charles Schwab to come back as CEO. Upon his return, Schwab declared that the company had "lost touch" with its heritage, and he promptly launched a restructuring program. To run the program, he enlisted Goldman, who shared his view that Schwab had drifted away from its roots. Recalling the period, Goldman told us, "The metrics around the decline were obvious. The customer statistics were falling, our stock price was plummeting, and we were losing market share. Our prices had crept up, and instead of looking at how to return to our strength and become competitive again, we began to convince ourselves that the answer lay in diversifying from our core and in finding ways to defend our high prices. Both ideas proved to be wrong."

Like Norwegian Cruise Line and The Home Depot, Schwab managed to survive its crisis of growth with a return to the founder's mentality. In chapter 5, we'll explore exactly how.

What the Data Shows about Value Creation during the Three Crises of Growth

These three crises of growth—overload, stall-out, and free fall—represent moments of powerful uncertainty, when companies need to take action to preserve momentum or prevent disaster. If not addressed, they can destroy huge amounts of value. But here's the good news: they also represent a major opportunity. If properly addressed, each can be leveraged into a moment of huge value creation.

When we recently reviewed the twenty-five biggest value swings that we've encountered through our work at Bain, we discovered a remarkable fact: every case involved a company facing one of these three crises. Why? Usually, it's because a sustained increase or decrease in a company's growth expectations (which can be fragile) triggers big swings in value (you can see this in the examples throughout this book).

To look at this process more systematically, we identified twenty companies that we knew well and that had a long history of value creation or of ups and downs, and looked at their last thirty years. As best we could, we separated the swings in value into two parts: (1) those where companies were in the midst of one of our three crises, and (2) times when they were not (steady-state growth, periods of multiple acquisitions, periods of diversification). The result: about 80 percent (and the largest spikes) of big value-creation swings occurred during the three crises.

You can see quite clearly in figure 2-2 that the biggest swings, accounting for a majority of all the value created, occur during the "journey north"—the insurgent period when a young company is trying to build the capacity to scale its business five or even ten times to be a major and sustained player in its industry. The second-largest swings occur during the later phase of a company's growth cycle, when free fall has started to set in.

To connect the chart in figure 2-2 to our three predictable crises, think of overload as the crisis that insurgents must overcome to increase or maintain their growth (the insurgent bar), think of stall-out as a major challenge of incumbency (the incumbent bar), and think of free fall as a very complex period with wide oscillations in value and outcome (three bars: late maturity, renewal, and continued decline). We made this latter separation for several reasons. First, we wanted to highlight the wide range of value swings that we observed. Second, we wanted to separate out companies grappling with impending free fall, companies that have successfully renewed themselves, and those that were not able to do so.

FIGURE 2-2

Rates of value creation during different phases of companies' life cycles

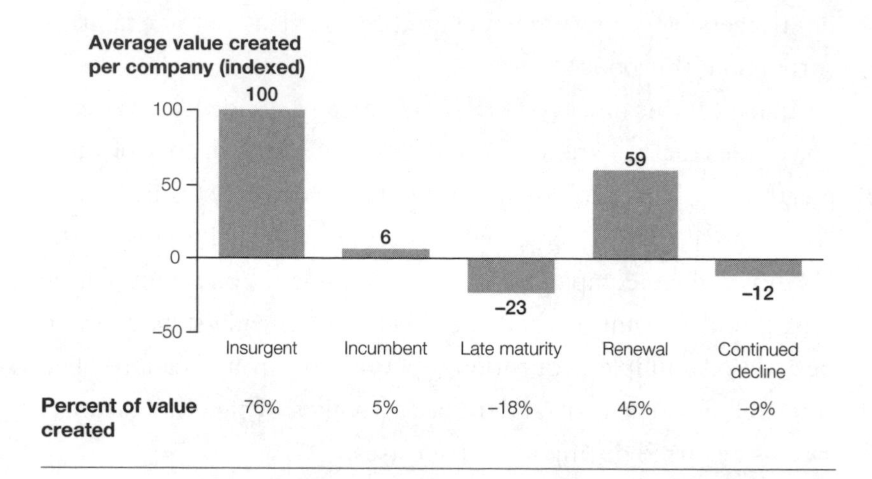

What the Data Shows about How These Three Internal Crises Interact with the External Challenges Companies Face

We began this book talking about the paradox of growth—how success in scaling a business on the outside can release forces on the inside that inhibit the next wave of profitable growth or even reverse momentum. This does not mean that companies do not face challenges from competitors or customers with new needs, or from new technologies. On the contrary, well over half of all businesses today face at least one form of significant outside disruption to a part of their business model or market in the form of a substitute product or service, a major shift in the profit drivers of the industry, or a fundamental change in customer needs or buying behaviors. But when we do case studies, reflect on our own experiences at Bain, interview management teams, or survey executives, we find that more than four in five problems on the outside of a business trace to problems on the inside—problems that inhibited its ability to adapt, to decide and act quickly, to embrace new ideas, to keep costs down, or to scale its ability to serve customers. The plot lines inside and outside ultimately have to converge, of course: you cannot win sustainably on the outside if you are losing internally, and vice versa. This is even true in free fall, as we will illustrate in chapter 5, where we will explore the cases of not only Charles Schwab but also DaVita and Crown Castle.

Figure 2-3 summarizes two of the surveys in which we asked a sample of executives about their perceived barriers to growth.

The first set of results shown in the figure derives from our survey of 325 executives worldwide about their growth challenges; the second set, from the executives who attended our FM100 workshops in developing markets. What we saw in our research is that executives cited internal barriers to growth four times as often as external ones. Executives cited internal barriers to growth about five times as often as an external lack of opportunities to obtain new sources of profitable growth. Furthermore, a remarkable 94 percent of barriers cited by large-company executives had their roots in internal dysfunction and lack of internal capabilities.

So what are these internal barriers? In overload, they involve predictable forces that we call the *westward winds*, because of how they push companies west into the upper-left quadrant of our map. In stall-out, they involve a set of predictable forces that we call the *southward winds*, because of how they push incumbents south into the bottom-left quadrant of the map. And in free fall, they involve systemic dysfunction on the inside that prevents companies from being able to adapt to profound strategic challenges on the outside—what we call *storms*, often

FIGURE 2-3

Barriers to profitable growth are both internal and external, and the internal ones are harder for leaders to manage

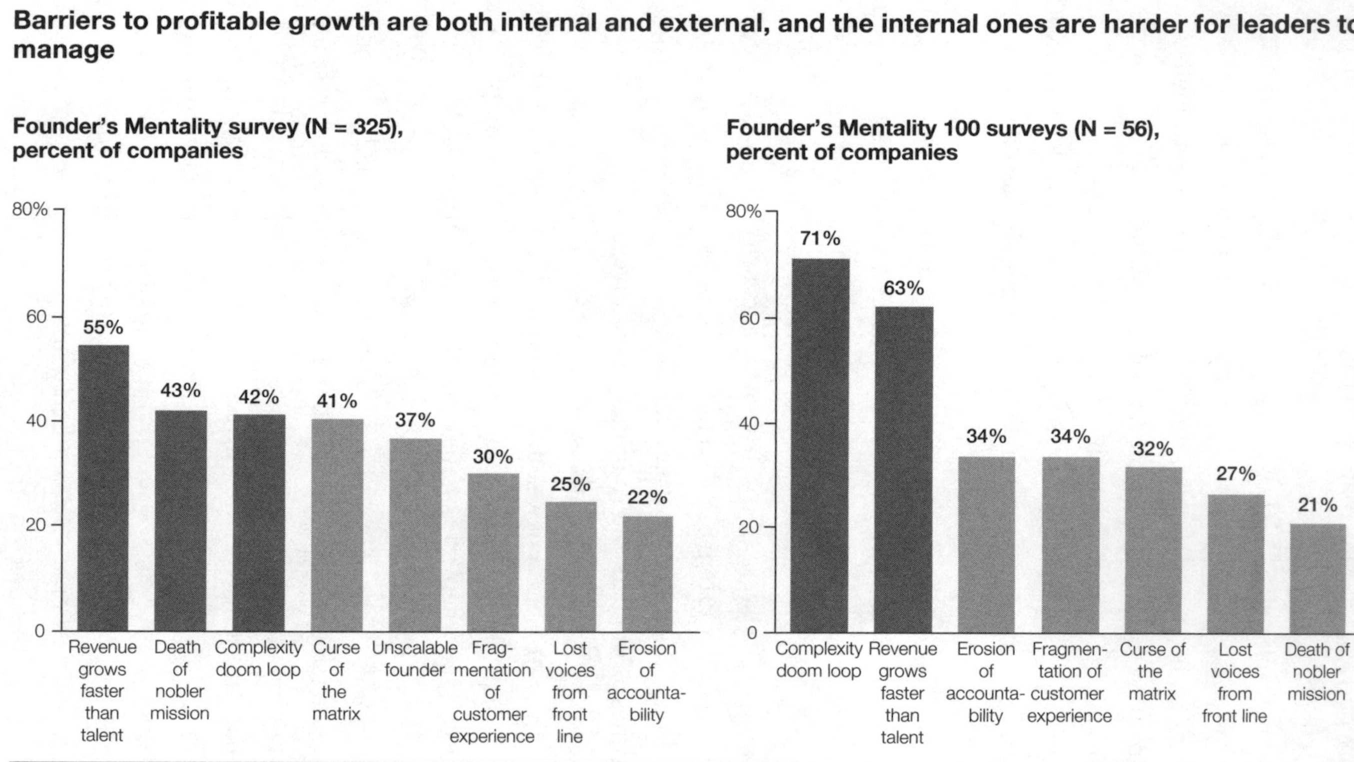

relating to the obsolescence of part of the business model itself. The example of Nokia, mentioned in our introduction, would be a classic example, exactly the type of "business disruption" Clayton Christensen identifies and discusses in his classic work on disruption.[8]

Now let's get more specific.

The Westward Winds: Overload and the Erosion of the Founder's Mentality

Growing a new business successfully involves pursuing the benefits of scale while staying true to the founder's mentality. This is the essence of what we've been calling the journey north: the move from insurgency at the bottom-right of our map, to scale insurgency at the top-right. To make that journey successfully, however, companies need to anticipate and make plans to cope with the westward winds: the internal forces that can blow them off course. We've identified four of them, as shown in figure 2-4, which we'll now briefly introduce one by one.

The Unscalable Founder

Everybody knows the type: the committed founder who finds himself out of his depth as his company grows but who simply can't let go, creating a bottleneck that impedes growth. Our research indicates that this problem afflicts one in three growing companies, and research on initial public offerings has shown that it can dramatically reduce the average return on investment. When we've talked to leaders who have experienced a major struggle in their journeys north, about two in five have listed the unscalable founder as a root cause.[9]

FIGURE 2-4

The westward winds

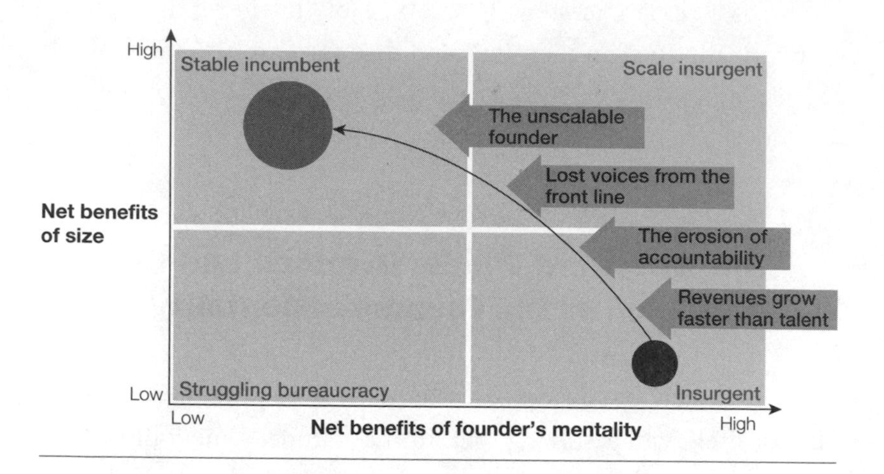

Lost Voices from the Front Line

When successful insurgent companies find themselves hit with the rapid-fire demands of overload, their managers often react in ways that put distance between themselves and the front line, and this, in turn, creates a westward drift away from the benefits of the founder's mentality.

The Erosion of Accountability

Accountability erodes surprisingly often during overload. Blinded by new layers of bureaucracy and complexity, and struggling to keep up with the short-term demands of growth, leaders and managers make decisions without direct accountability. Forty-six percent of the 325 executives we interviewed believed that they had experienced erosion in the founder's mentality because of dysfunctional and unaccountable decision making—a process that can stop a company in its tracks.

Revenues Grow Faster Than Talent

As the pace of their growth increases, companies often begin to make errors and accumulate debris that ultimately will kill them. Nowhere is this more apparent than with hiring. As successful insurgents attempt to manage their own burgeoning complexity, they make staffing errors. At the top level, they hire professionals with large-company expertise who make dramatic, disruptive changes to the founding culture. Throughout the company, they staff up with great speed, and in doing so, they often sacrifice employee quality for quantity. Soon employees lose touch with the company's original mission and principles, they turn their gaze inward and lose focus on the front lines, and they become thinkers more than doers.

The Southward Winds: Reversing the Benefits of Scale

Many executives seem bewildered by the painful slowdown that comes with incumbency. But they have no trouble describing the symptoms:

> We've lost touch with customers. We've become too bureaucratic. We're drowning in process and PowerPoint presentations. We have the resources and no shortage of opportunities, but somehow we've lost the ability or the will to make the most of them. Everything's complicated, and everybody's tired. Competitors seem faster than they used to be, and we can't make decisions or mobilize quickly enough. A good day at the office used to involve making decisions and taking action, but now it means attending a big meeting of department heads, whose focus might

be "creating alignment around strategy" or achieving a quarter-point increase return on average weighted capital. Running the business—once such a personal, high-energy ride—now feels like flying a huge, sluggish airliner. We've lost touch with what got us into the business in the first place, and we no longer know where we're going beyond the annual budget, nor do we know where new growth will come from.

These are effects of the southward winds, which we've summed up in figure 2-5. They create internal complexity, they weaken and slow down decision making, they depersonalize the customer experience, and they erode or obscure the core mission, which leads to employees' disillusionment and lack of engagement.

FIGURE 2-5

The southward winds

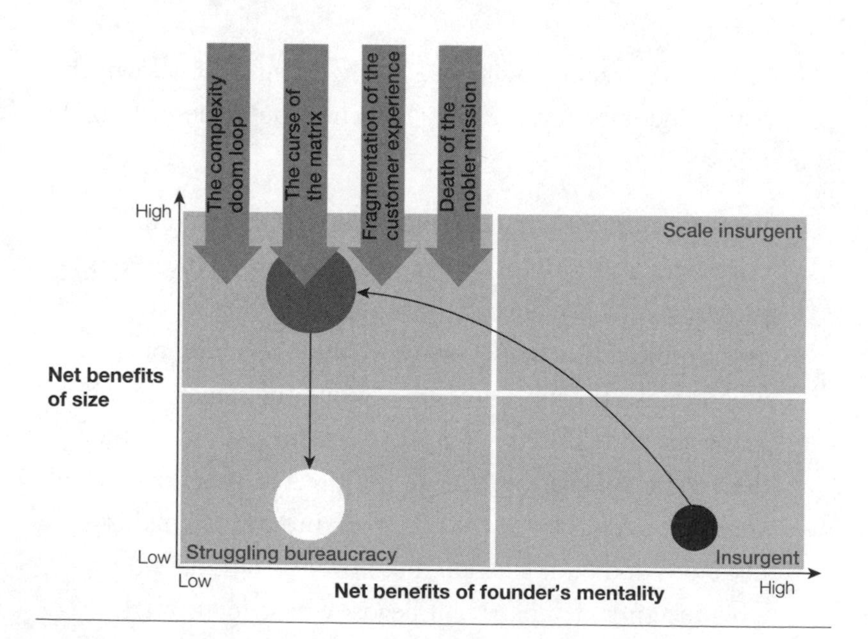

Together, the southward winds can transform the power of incumbency into the vulnerability of bureaucracy, and they sap the life out of a company and the energy out of its people. They threaten to make it stall out.

Let's now look at them one by one.

The Complexity Doom Loop

Every business begins with a single product, a single segment, and a single way of going to market. Then growth begins, bringing new opportunities, new customer segments, new geographies, new product lines, new businesses, new channels of distribution, and new services. These are the bright, shiny objects of business: they provide immediate gratification and energy. Yet they also add complexity, and that leads to what we call the complexity doom loop: unchecked complexity silently kills growth and sucks energy from the organization, creating tired leaders. And tired leaders become distracted from their key mission of translating strategy into simple actions and routines at the front line of the business.

Complexity doesn't have to be a negative. Incumbents are multinational businesses with complex product portfolios, after all, geared to serve complex customer needs. Managed effectively, that can actually be a competitive advantage. Consumer goods companies that can efficiently serve the complex needs of multinational retailers gain a crucial edge on those that can't. Construction companies adept at delivering bespoke solutions to solve convoluted customer demands can command higher margins.

Complexity, a central villain in this book, is obviously not homogeneous. It differs within and among organizations, and needs to be attacked at a variety of different levels. But here's the point: to survive the southward winds, companies need to make complexity reduction a way of life.

Companies that do this have flatter organizations that put leadership closer to the customers, better maintain the founder's mentality, and achieve more sustained profitability. Steve Jobs recognized this. That's why, on his return to rejuvenate Apple, he focused first on the reduction of complexity in organization (he consolidated some departments), in product line (he eliminated 70 percent), in research (reduced to a handful of projects), in design (simplicity became a mantra again), and in the supply base (the number of suppliers was cut from a hundred to twenty-four). "People think being focused means saying yes to a thing that you have to focus on," he said in 1997, at the Worldwide Developers Conference held annually by Apple. "But that's not what it means at all. It means saying no to the hundred other good ideas that are out there. You have to pick carefully. I'm actually as proud of the things we haven't done as the things we've done."

The Curse of the Matrix

Large, mature businesses often successfully run themselves as "matrix" organizations. These are companies in which responsibility is formally assigned to managers in cross-cutting slices of the organization, in functions (finance or sales), geographies (countries or regions), customer segments (government or small business), or product areas (hardware, software, or services).

The problem is that in matrix organizations, departmental priorities can blur the sense of collective purpose—the insurgent mission that's so important to the founder's mentality. As the matrix grows, so does bureaucracy. Internal politics consume more time and energy than ever. Nodes of interaction develop between middle managers and the people at each node whose only job, it sometimes appears, is to say no. The founder's clarity—the notion that there are those who sell and those who support those who sell—gets lost in a sea of competing interests. We call all of this the "curse of the matrix."

Successful organizations need to make good decisions and to coordinate actions fast. But the curse of the matrix works against that and, in doing so, makes stall-out a real possibility. One of our colleagues studied a large organization mired in bureaucratic sluggishness. He tabulated the number of hours that the company's employees were collectively devoting per year to the weekly executive meeting, not only in attending it but also in coordinating departments, setting agendas, preparing reports, and so on. The total astonished everybody: 300,000 hours. One meeting, 300,000 hours![10]

Inevitably, applying the matrix organizational structure to a growing company will lead to internal conflict. The problem is how conflict gets resolved. Insurgents understand this, and their bias for action and their obsession with the front line ensure that conflict doesn't bog down the organization. But incumbents learn to hate internal conflict. Why?

First, they let conflict become personal. Employees in different parts of the organization lose their sense of perspective. They let general debates about how best to serve customers become personal fights. This means one employee or department has to "win" and the other has to "lose," and this outcome produces shock waves that reverberate far beyond the specific decision being debated.

Second, they start to consider conflict "unprofessional." Big organizations create processes that seem to be more about time management than customer issues, and so don't like it when employees energetically start a conflict and take the meetings "off track or off schedule." They want the agenda and decorum to rule.

Third, they let the energy vampires take over. Anyone who has worked in companies on the verge of bureaucracy will recognize the energy vampires right away. They schedule lots of meetings. They exercise pocket vetoes on key decisions and delay action with their requests for one more round of analytics. They send out a lot of templates. You hate it when they appear on your calendar. They wait at the other end of e-mail, ready to fire off missives that force your people to stop serving the customer and instead respond to yet another information request. Rather than breaking problems down into bite-sized chunks that people can take away and act on, they raise high-level issues that can't be solved. They force everybody to fight shadow battles under the surface. They kill organizations like strangler vines.

The curse of the matrix even causes many companies to lose access to their own resources. Why? Resources in matrix organizations get trapped in departmental silos, often defended by ballooning central staffs that have become the ultimate experts at the internal game. This slows down decision making and makes it impossible to concentrate resources. Big companies that have lost the founder's mentality tend to spread resources around evenly, an understandable instinct, but one that leads inevitably to mediocrity. Great founders work differently: often willing to invest overwhelming resources on a new capability or to deal with a crisis, they allocate their resources very selectively. Their approach isn't smooth, it's spiky.

Fragmentation of the Customer Experience

Everybody knows this problem. You call a big company with a question, but nobody seems to really want to help. Your experience as a customer is fragmented and depersonalized. Nobody actually "owns" your problem, and each employee you deal with seems eager to move you on to someone else. You get transferred on the phone from one person to another, always ineffectually.

Everybody you talk to seems to care only about their little corner of the organization and wants to get you off the phone to rack up the total call-handled numbers. Nobody cares broadly about the whole. Nobody is accountable to *you* or for *you*. The case of The Home Depot, described earlier, is a perfect example of this problem and the consequences of not addressing it.

Death of the Nobler Mission

The executives we've interviewed about maintaining the founder's mentality as their companies grow cite one factor more than any other: a tight, intense focus on principles and purpose. Lose the shared sense of nobler mission that animated your insurgency, they all agree, and you lose your company's soul.

This is not a touchy-feely concern. Employee engagement with a nobler mission translates into behaviors that create success externally, because it causes people to go the extra mile for the company, for the customer, or for fellow employees. One study found that engaged employees are 4.7 times more likely than the average to recommend the company to a friend, 3.5 times more likely to make suggestions about how to improve the business, and 3.5 times more likely to take initiative to do something positive that was not expected of them.[11] When some of our Bain colleagues looked at this phenomenon in front-line call centers, they found that the most engaged employees take accountability to a higher level, give out their contact information for follow-up, and demonstrate more empathy toward the customer. Management teams ignore these factors at their peril.

The story of Hewlett-Packard, one of the true founders of Silicon Valley, illustrates the importance of these principles and shows what can happen when they are negated. Bill Hewlett and David Packard founded the company in 1938 with a very clear idea of the kind of company they were trying to build. "We wanted to avoid a bureaucracy," Packard wrote in *The HP Way*, "and create a company where the problem-solving solutions would be made as close as possible to the level at which it occurred." Not only that, he continued, "Bill and I had no desire to see HP become a conglomerate. More companies die from indigestion than starvation."[12]

Hewlett and Packard exuded the founder's mentality, and their focus on organic growth and the primacy of the engineer carried the company far. But starting in 1999, the first in a series of externally hired CEOs took the company in a different direction and bulked up the business with acquisitions, including, in 2002, the computer giant Compaq. Walter Hewlett, Bill's son, hated what was happening and published an open letter to HP stockholders in the *Wall Street Journal*, in which he expressed his fears about the "loss of both focus and strategic clarity," and about "clashes of culture and poor employee morale."[13]

He was right to be worried. Four CEOs later, HP's stock price underperformed the Dow Jones Industrial Average index by about 50 percent during that time. This was not the only reason for the company's stall-out, but it was certainly an important factor. As the *Harvard Business Review* said of the company in 2011, "It has lost the 'HP Way'—the values and behaviors and principles and commitments that made it more than *just another company* [italics added]."[14] That's the particularly insidious danger of this southward wind: it makes you lose a sense of your mission and direction, and turns you into just another company.

In the chapters ahead, we'll be discussing all of this in greater detail. For now, though, we'll just reiterate a key point: the three crises of growth—overload, stall-out, and free fall—are central to about 80 percent of major swings in value, up and down, for the average company during its lifetime. How you handle these crises *matters*. So let's now turn to how a variety of leaders and their teams have coped with these crises, and to how they've relied on the founder's mentality to help them succeed.

USING THE FOUNDER'S MENTALITY IN YOUR ORGANIZATION

✓ Schedule a dozen workshops across the organization to discuss:

- Where is your business located on the founder's mentality map and which winds are hurting you most?
- How are these forces reducing your ability to respond to customers and compete with speed and robbing your people of their energy and freedom to act?
- What actions can you start taking now to restore the founder's mentality and what measures can you use to check your progress?
- What capabilities are missing or are not strong enough to keep your company competitive in the future? What actions can you take to acquire or strengthen them?

✓ What can leaders do on their own, independent of an institutional response?

3

Combating Overload

How the Founder's Mentality Overcomes the Chaos of High Growth

Most founders fail. The numbers are large—hundreds of thousands per year. Early failure usually comes because the business idea didn't fly high enough to attract continued funding and justify growing it. But we're not writing about those companies here. Our focus is on the survivors: the few start-ups that get significant traction. One reward for their success is the right to proceed to the next level of the game—and that's where they confront overload (see figure 3-1).

So what do you do when overload hits? To answer this question, let's return to the story of Norwegian Cruise Line, which we began in the previous chapter. It's the story of a company that ran aground, despite a strong position in a growing market, and

FIGURE 3-1

Fighting the crisis of overload

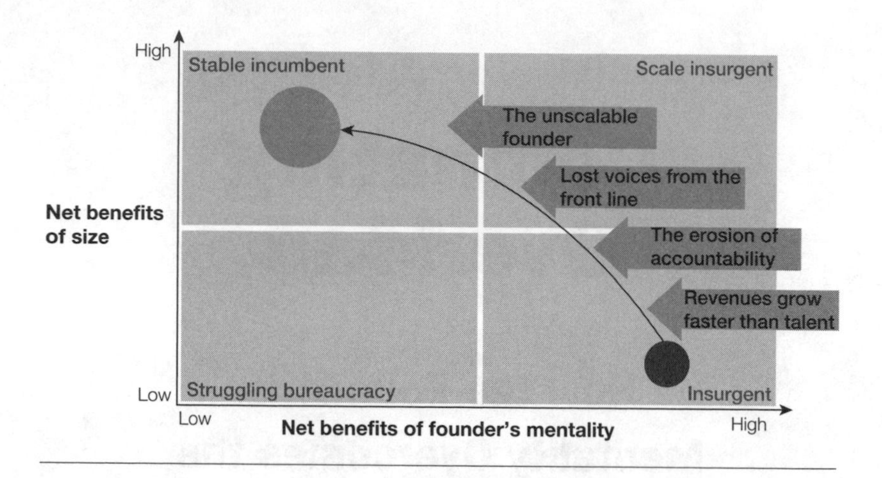

reversed its course by rebuilding from the front line up while sharpening its insurgent mission.

The Power of the Founder's Mentality

When we left off, the company's new CEO, Kevin Sheehan, had just taken over and was realizing that he had a real mess on his hands. A victim of its own rapid growth, Norwegian had been blown off course by the westward winds, and Sheehan's job was to get the company back on track, headed once again for scale insurgency.

Sheehan acted fast. During his first year with Norwegian, he changed more than 80 percent of the company's top-tier executives, looked for ways to rediscover the company's core mission, and began the work of transformation from the front line up. This involved a number of key learning initiatives rooted in the power of the founder's mentality, among them the following:

Opening up lines of communication. One of the central dysfunctions that plagued Norwegian during its decline was that shipside personnel didn't believe that shoreside personnel understood the challenges of their work, and vice versa. Sheehan made connecting these two sides a key priority. To make sure each learned from the other, he and his team began including shipside staff in processes and decisions that had previously been handled exclusively in the corporate office, and invited officers from across the fleet to attend the company's leadership retreats.

Celebrating and rewarding front-line heroes. Sheehan and his team introduced what they called the Vacation Hero program, which taught employees how to better engage guests and identified employees who had gone out of their way to make a passenger's stay special or to solve a problem. The emphasis in this program was on sharing knowledge within the company to better serve customers.

Making constant improvement a focus. Company leaders put in place a kaizen (or continuous improvement) system to gather ideas from the front line on how to improve and streamline operations and processes everywhere in the organization, and created extensive discussion forums and recognition for the best ideas. They even developed a method to involve employees in the details of ship design, a powerful example of their new emphasis on the vertical rather than the horizontal.

Codifying best practices. The company developed a new software program, delivered through iPads, that defined and gathered inputs on Platinum Standards—that is, the best practices in terms of both operations and passenger loyalty drivers.

Keeping staff focused on core principles and customer needs. To make this happen, the leadership team delivered what it called Freestyle Fundamentals to staff: daily tips for customer-facing staff to think about each day.

Introducing measures of employee engagement, partner satisfaction, and customer advocacy. Norwegian put such measures in place for each ship and each cruise, and has made improvement in each category a priority. We've checked the numbers ourselves and can attest that they show a consistent increase.

Sheehan's transformation of Norwegian is a true success story. In early 2013, the company went public and became one of the most successful IPOs of the year, closing the year 87 percent above its IPO price. From 2008 through 2013, EBITDA margins increased for twenty consecutive quarters, from 5 percent to 25 percent. Revenues have grown by 50 percent since Sheehan took over, and measures of health such as net yield and average fleet age are now the best in the industry (see figure 3-2).

We asked Sheehan to reflect on the turnaround. Recalling the state of the company when he took over, he said, "We were unfocused, operations were sloppy, and it was putting huge strain on our employees. Nothing seemed repeatable across ships or cruises or shore relationships. In five years, we changed all that and now have the basis for a unique and repeatable business model built around Freestyle Cruising that we can apply over and over."

The crisis of overload is stressful because it usually happens when people are working as hard as they have ever worked in their lives, with limited capacity to deal with more, in pursuit of something they care about a lot. The first signs of overload are bottlenecks, things falling through the cracks, systems that

FIGURE 3-2

The renewal of Norwegian Cruise Line

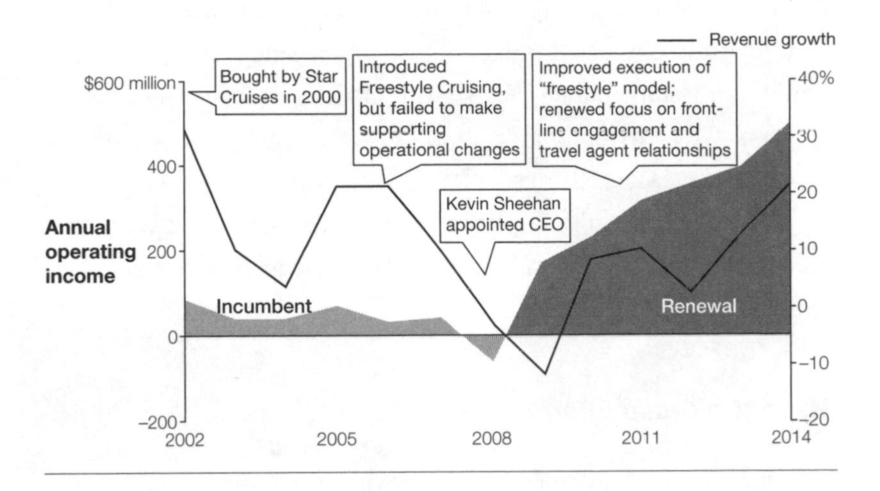

are not scaling, talent stretched to the breaking point, increasing tension among colleagues, and maybe even the first onset of organizational malaise and loss of confidence; it then ripples to the outside in terms of sub-par performance in the marketplace, customer frustrations, and financial shortfalls. A helpful image to keep in mind is that of a plate spinner. In overload, the spinner has to set more and more plates in motion, and then keep them in motion. Quickly, what had been a satisfying process of growth (more plates) becomes a troubling one: plates start to wobble, the spinner can't keep them all in motion, and they begin to fall to the floor. The spinner's mission now changes: no longer is it to serve and delight his audience (customers); it's merely to cope with this crisis of growth and avoid catastrophe.

Let's turn now to some general ways in which companies have used the founder's mentality to prevent or mitigate the crisis of overload.

Building the Insurgency

There can be little of greater importance to a growing company than its unique reason for existing, its insurgency, and the expansion that mission enables. Yet, despite its importance, a sharp definition of what the company stands for and what makes it special is one of the easiest things to let drift in the crush of daily to-do lists and overscheduled agendas. Here are some of the ways that successful leaders have maintained the insurgency as they have scaled their businesses.

Make It a Group Effort

Let's start with the case of Harsh Mariwala, the founder and CEO of Marico, a consumer-products company in India. Mariwala started his consumer product journey in the early 1970s with a single product line—edible oils. Annual revenues then were just $8,000 per year—or $15,000 at current exchange rates. By any measure, the odds were stacked against Marico. But Mariwala thought there was room to grow.

To give but one instance, edible coconut oil was then sold in fifteen-liter tins. After much deliberation, he introduced Indians to smaller and more convenient plastic containers. These were designed so that pests like rats couldn't gnaw through them.

In doing this, he achieved two things. First, he made an otherwise unwieldy product accessible to the masses in an easy-to-store form. Second, he drove down prices of what had been a luxury product until even those at the bottom of the pyramid could afford it.

This innovation in place, he traveled throughout rural India and started to build a mind-boggling distribution network of three million outlets. The outcome was there for all to see. Even the remotest villages started to stock Marico's products. Between these innovations and distribution network, the brand soon became a source of competitive advantage and fueled the company's resurgence.

Marico is now the largest hair-oil company in the world. It controls a significant market share and occupies the number-one position in 90 percent of the segments it operates in. A robust overseas franchise brings in 25 percent of its revenues. The company now has a market value of over $4 billion and during the last fifteen years has maintained revenue growth of 15 percent and profit growth of 20 percent.

Part of his success, Mariwala told us, stemmed from actions he took to embed Marico's strategy and principles when the company had five hundred employees and forty managers on its rolls. With managers coming in from different organizations, everybody had his own views on how the business should be run. "It started to get chaotic," he said.

> I realized that to manage properly, I had to define what we stand for. So I started to codify it on how people ought to treat each other in the company and what our culture should be. When I was done, the document was about forty pages long and covered people, products, strategy, customers, our view of the markets, and how we ought to look at profits.
>
> I shared this with the team, and the response was positive. No one had seen something like this in firms where they worked earlier. But I soon realized this was my view. It had to become theirs as well. So we initiated a process with the top few layers of the company to discuss, modify, and operationalize it. We gathered inputs and refined our thinking in about twelve full days of discussions across

> a year. When we were done with it, we had a document on hand with three sections in it: People, Products, and Profits.
>
> We then went to the next layer of employees and went on an offsite to discuss and refine it further. This level of discussion was important to create ownership, eliminate cynicism, and drive an understanding that this is how we intend to run the business—and that these are not just words on paper.
>
> We did this all across the company. It defined what is right and acceptable and what is not. Our priorities and goals were in it as well. We then worked hard to create policies and procedures to make these real, enforce, and embed them. It proved to be a document that empowered people closer to the front line to take action themselves, as long as their actions were consistent with our principles and values.

Mariwala and his team made sure every element of the document they had labored on for over a year led to actions that changed daily procedures to run the company. Take a value Marico calls "openness." To emphasize this value, Mariwala created an office where employees could all see one another and didn't have to go through an assistant to talk to the CEO.

To reinforce this value further, Mariwala initiated open house meetings. He'd visit every office and factory, and make himself available for hours to employees who had questions. He also initiated training programs focused on values and started to reward and celebrate people for reinforcing them.

He worked hard to minimize hierarchy as well. In many Indian organizations, supervisors and senior executives are typically addressed as Sir or Ma'am. Mariwala insisted that employees at all levels be called "members" and address one another by their first names.

Looking back, Mariwala says that codifying, socializing, and embedding purpose at the company's core—and relying on everybody to do the same—is what lies at the heart of Marico's success. His achievements are impressive. Today, Marico employs about 2,400 people, and its stock price has increased twelvefold over the last decade.

Leaders in rapidly growing companies need to set aside enough time to ensure that everyone understands and feels connected to the purpose of the company, including involving them directly in shaping it. In chapter 5, we'll consider the extreme version of this strategy: the complete "refounding" of a company, as exemplified by DaVita, which between 1999 and 2015 went from near bankruptcy to being the best-performing health-care company of the decade.

Disrupt Your Own Insurgency

In chapter 1, we told the story of Yonghui, the Chinese grocery business, to illustrate the importance of having a clear, insurgent mission. But the company has other lessons to teach about how to harness the power of the founder's mentality. It has been very successful, for example, in disrupting its *own* insurgency.

Let's explain what we mean. The company's founders, the Zhang brothers, disrupted Chinese retail with their original stores, which they ran themselves. But as they scaled the company, they realized they needed to bring in and carefully integrate professional managers to take those stores to the next level and make them their primary, stable engine of growth. They called these stores their "red stores." At the same time, they recognized the ways in which professionalization and more-complex systems opened their business up to disruption from smaller, nimbler, insurgent competitors. So they decided to build a second set of stores in which employees could focus on innovation, without the burdens of managing the increasingly large and complex red stores. They called these new stores their "green stores," and their reason for being was simple. As one of the brothers, Xuanning, told us, "We either disrupt ourselves or leave it to others."

He explained the approach in detail:

> Our insurgent mission is simple: safe, fresh, good-value food for the Chinese mother. We have stood for this since we opened our first store. To deliver that mission demands we focus on our supply chain. We need to source high-quality food from trusted suppliers and deliver this food fresh to our customers every day—not always that easy to do in rural China. As we grow, expanding our stores and product range, the importance of our supply chain at the center of our competitive advantage also grows. So you'd think it would be clear to all—while we want to improve everywhere, what really matters is our supply chain. This is where we must "spike."
>
> We are still a young company, going through a transition from two young brothers barely able to manage the chaos of growth, to a more professional organization. We are bringing in outside experts, from finance to HR, from pricing to category management. We need this. But what we have learned the hard way is that each professional has their agenda based on their past experience that creates lots of expert voices competing against our supply-chain agenda. How do you keep focus on *the* critical capability in a company building lots of capabilities through lots of initiatives? We can run around the company and shout, "It's all about the supply chain! It's all about the supply chain!" But, of

> course, our people have already heard that. So they can easily get seduced by the next shiny toy. One of the jobs of the leader is to keep the organization really focused on the one or two things that matter above all else.

This leads to the second part of the story. One of the main reasons the brothers shifted management responsibilities for their red stores to professionals was that they wanted to shift their attention to what they do best—starting new businesses and innovating. They wanted to stay in touch with the founder's mentality as their company grew.

Xuanning described the ongoing challenge. "Growth is getting harder as our industry becomes more saturated and more competitive," he said. "My brother and I realized we must continue to be the innovators. We did it once with our 'red-store format'—what we call our original-store model. But we need to do more, hence, our 'green-store format.' These are our incubators for innovation. If the 'red stores' want to adopt a green-store innovation, they are welcome to do so, but they cannot constrain green-store innovation, even if that innovation might hurt red-store sales. While always painful, this is a good thing and keeps our insurgency alive."

Embedding Front-Line Obsession

An organization is ahead of the game in preventing overload if its front-line employees love the details of the business and feel empowered to solve tactical problems on the spot. Organizations that work this way create more capacity to grow and keep decision processes swift and smooth. Their employees are more loyal and productive, and the result is a self-correcting organization that learns and changes almost automatically. Here are some ways in which we have seen successful companies accomplish this.

Put the Front Line First

In our FM100 workshops worldwide, we ask every audience of CEOs about their biggest growth barriers. And what they point to most frequently is their inability to hire, retain, and grow the capabilities of employees at the front line of the business and at the most pivotal operational points. We have talked with the leaders in a wide range of companies that have effectively overcome this problem. Here are a few examples.

Let's start with Oberoi Hotels, whose story we began telling in chapter 1. When we visited Vikram Oberoi, the group CEO, we asked him about the company's talent management. "We never select for a specific position," he told us, "but select on a few fundamental traits, including that everyone we hire has the potential to grow at least two levels up in the organization. We begin to think of people's long-term paths right at the start, which creates a greater sense of mutual commitment." To that end, Oberoi doesn't limit itself geographically when hiring. When the Oberoi Hotel in Jaipur was hiring for its opening, the management team visited eighteen cities to staff the hotel over a period of forty-two days, reviewing nearly nine thousand applications for only about two hundred positions. During the interviews, the team didn't look for technical skills, but for personal values and a track record of being, as Vikram Oberoi put it, "driven, hungry, and really wanting to succeed."

From the point of hire on, everything at Oberoi is designed to make employees feel a sense of long-term commitment. Within three months of their hiring, employees are invited individually to a special meal with management in the hotel restaurant; their families are invited, too, and everybody who comes, Vikram Oberoi told us, is "made to feel like royalty." After six months with Oberoi, employees receive their "confirmation": a rite of passage that includes photos with their team sent to their family to celebrate their progress.

Trust is a key value at Oberoi. Remarkably, even junior employees have access to such information as financial results and hotel performance with customers. Nearly all management meetings are open to any employees who want to sit in on them. Everything—from how reviews are done, to kudo cards that any employee can give out, to awards for people who deserve special recognition, to role modeling humble behaviors—traces back to the practices of the founder.

Balance Heroes and Systems

Insurgent companies thrive on heroics, epitomized by the many amazing Horatio Alger stories of the great founders. But eventually they need to grow up. They have to add new expertise, capabilities, and systems to bring order to the chaos of rapid growth, the unsustainable hours, the lack of control. They have to professionalize. Too often, however, professionalization can take on a life of its own or devolve into an exercise of mimicking the very incumbents they are attacking. Here are some ideas for how to reduce that risk.

Ensure that the professionalization agenda is set by the strategic agenda. The job seems obvious. Of course the strategic agenda should set the professionalization agenda, right? The problem is that as an insurgent company professionalizes, it adds functions, and each new function comes with a new leader and a new staff determined to improve that function. This creates a growing collection of disparate functional agendas that can quickly overwhelm a company and cause it to lose focus. Many of our FM100 meetings have focused on this. At one meeting, a founder (who has chosen to remain anonymous) told us a particularly illustrative story:

> My first step was to recognize I had a big problem. I had brought in a half-dozen managers to help professionalize my company, but after a while I couldn't even understand what was being discussed at our management meetings. The head of HR would stand up and talk about HR excellence and outline a ten-step program to bring us up to a world-class standard. Then our head of supply chain would do the same, but he called his program "In pursuit of functional excellence." Our management meetings became long report-outs of all these ten-step programs, and we stopped talking about the customer or what we were trying to do to change our industry. So I told everybody to stop. I asked each of our functional heads to come back with the two or three things they were going to do to support our insurgent mission, and that mission only. Two weeks later, we met as a team and reviewed their work. Now I could see the connection between our strategy, our capability-building program, and our professionalization agenda. And the most surprising thing was that our functional heads all thanked me. They finally had clarity and focus on what they were doing and felt far more connected to the business.

This last point is critical. When they arrive at insurgent companies, professionals usually want to do the right thing. But they get little direction. Because the founding team is unsure how to professionalize, they are reluctant to give the experts direction. But the story just told shows what the founding team can do: they can help newly arrived professionals link their agenda to the insurgent mission. This provides much-needed focus and integrates them much more tightly into the company.

This brings us to another important job in managing heroes and systems: overriding systems. The risk-reduction ideas that follow all offer ways for leadership teams to stay fast and sharp as their processes become more complex and impersonal.[1]

Commit to Monday meetings. One way you can ensure a balance between heroes and systems as you pursue rapid growth is by implementing a "Monday meeting." We are not, by the way, suggesting that businesses have more large, internal meetings. On the contrary, what we are describing is one particular type of meeting that can have the effect of reducing work and increasing the metabolism of a business. The simple idea is for leaders of the company to meet once a week with a promise: at this meeting, no matter how long it takes, they will work to unblock any obstacle that is preventing key players from doing their jobs.

A meeting of this sort (which doesn't have to happen on Mondays) has four immediate benefits. First, it signals to the whole organization that the problem-solving cadence of the company is now four days. Leaders can no longer blame the organization (or new systems and processes) for delays. Second, it forces the leadership team to talk in an integrated way about the problems that are making it hard for key players to get their jobs done. Leaders can't hide. Third, the meetings keep the senior team action-oriented and reduce the cycle time from decision to action. Team members can't leave the meeting until they solve problems, so they learn to deconstruct problems and to make big issues small enough to be fixable, precisely the kind of bias to action that animates the founder's mentality.

Les Wexner has made the Monday meeting into one of the most important management routines at L Brands. It helps keep the cycle time of solving problems short, he told us, and removes blockages to action. The wrinkle at L Brands, which makes it an even more powerful management technique, is the Tuesday follow-up, a check-in on the progress of decisions and any new bottlenecks encountered. This strategy is employed by one of Wexner's most successful CEOs, Nick Coe, who runs Bath & Body Works and the new start-up White Barn. Coe attributes a lot of his success to these meetings. "The Monday and Tuesday meetings are company-wide, fifty-two weeks per year," he told us, "and you never miss it. It is the most disciplined thing we do. It has morphed to 'we can't live without it.' It is done for each business, no matter how new."

Another master of the Monday meeting is Galip Yorgancioğlu, the CEO of Mey Içki. The story of Mey, the leading spirits company in Turkey, is well known. For about sixty years, the Turkish government ran a state monopoly that manufactured and distributed all raki: the anise-oil-based spirit that is Turkey's national drink. Turks will sit for hours at their raki table ritual, drinking glasses of raki while nibbling at meze, a collection of small dishes of hot and cold food. When the government decided to privatize the industry in 2004, some construction entrepreneurs bought what would become Mey and set to work. They didn't know much about consumer goods, but knew enough to recruit Yorgancioğlu as their CEO. He was their first employee and remains in charge today. For good reason: the first owners bought the company for roughly $292 million and sold it to TPG Capital two years later for about $810 million. And then TPG sold it to Diageo for about $2.1 billion. That's an increase of ten times in value in about ten years—not a bad value-creation story.

We had the privilege of meeting with Yorgancioğlu and his sales and marketing directors in Istanbul. He is a massive proponent of the Monday meeting, when his leaders can get together and solve issues fast. He said:

> One of the hardest things to do culturally is to make everyone understand that conflict is okay. We build the possibility of conflict into our organizations, and the worst thing we can do is then avoid the inevitable conflict that arises. I want my supply-chain team to deliver to our consumers

> the benefits of "sameness." I want them fighting to rationalize, to look for scale benefits. And I want my marketing guys to deliver to our consumers the benefits of difference. I want them fighting for new variants, new products. And my job is to make sure that we address the conflicts that inevitably arise when our people are doing their job.
>
> One trick I've found to do this is what I call double hatting. When we first talk about an issue, I want each person to represent that organizational hat they've been assigned. So if you're in charge of supply chain, fight your corner. This makes sure we get the issues on the table and everyone understands that the conflicts we are raising are conflicts we want. Then I say, okay, now let's switch hats. We're all owners of the business; we now have all the issues on the table. What is the right answer? I now want people to debate the answer on behalf of the whole company.

Embracing conflict keeps Mey agile. "Speed and agility demands fast decision making," Yorgancioğlu told us. "Fast decision making demands that we get all the issues on the table and then make the right decision for our consumers and our company. The Monday meeting lets us do that. The whole company knows that we'll deal with the issues that come up each Monday, so they raise any issues that are stopping them from taking action. It's a social contract, and if we do it right, it ensures that we move faster than our competitors."

Draw lines in the sand. Probably the greatest insurgent growth story of the 1990s was the rise of Dell and its direct model for selling computers. During the high-growth phase, Michael Dell and his team identified four physical measures of health that they applied to each segment of the business (product, geography, customer) and to the business as a whole. Each was designed to be highly measurable, relevant to every level of the company, and require immediate action if they slipped. One of the measures, for example, was the percent of products slipped on time: a key profit driver, and a real line in the sand.

Create a council of franchise players. Every company can identify some employees, not necessarily department heads or people with big titles, who have a disproportionate impact on the performance of the company and its delivery to customers. We call these employees "franchise players." Examples might be the account manager for a customer who represents 25 percent of all sales, or the leading product developer. Creating a council of these franchise players lets a senior team cut through layers of bureaucracy and engage in an open dialogue directly with the most influential and perhaps highest-potential employees. One CEO we know has brought many small founder-led businesses into his company and holds periodic meetings with only their founders, who provide an animated and unique perspective on the company. Another CEO holds periodic sessions with what he calls his "high potentials" to stay in touch with some of the biggest influencers, not all of whom have big titles.

We could list many more tactics that help a growing insurgent company balance heroes and systems. But these three tactics—Monday meetings, lines in the sand, and giving special attention to franchise players—are among the most powerful. We've seen them implemented in many different situations and have witnessed their effectiveness firsthand.

Demanding an Owner's Mindset

The owner's mindset at its best is focused on the long term, has a strong bias to speed and action, and demands that personal responsibility guide business decisions and actions. Let's now look under the hood of several companies that have maintained their owner's mindset and ask how they have embedded this lasting source of strength.

Build a Lean and Hungry Organization

What does the owner's mindset really mean? What does it feel like? How can a large company embed it deeply in its employees and its culture? For answers, we turned to AB InBev, the world's largest beer company, whose story we introduced in chapter 1 ("We create restaurant owners, not waiters").

AB InBev has adopted a number of very visible approaches to embedding the owner's mindset. It demands that every budget item be defended in the open every year. It sets aggressive goals around the key profit drivers in every part of the business. It makes sure that leadership targets cascade down and are disaggregated to the next level of leaders, so that every person is clear how he or she connects to the whole; no one escapes, there is no place to hide, and all face challenging gaps to fill. AB InBev challenges key managers to dream up threats that could disrupt part of their business model, such as changes in packaging. It maintains a widely publicized list of ten core principles and their prominent use in the company.

Each of these programs has a significant role in maintaining the competitive intensity, amazing work ethic, and founder's mentality of AB InBev. But to get to the deeper answer of how AB InBev has maintained its edge as it has scaled so profoundly, you need to look deeper. And when you do, you find that the secret to the company's success—and to achieving scale insurgency in general—is the replication throughout the company of the core values and beliefs of the founder's mentality. The best analogy we can think of is the replication of plants from an original seed. That's what the image on the cover of this book symbolizes.

We spoke with Jo Van Biesbroeck, one of AB InBev's longest-serving employees, about this process. His roles at the company have included leading European operations, the export business of smaller countries, the finance department, the acquisition team, and, most recently, the strategy team. He explained to us a number of ways in which the process works at AB InBev:

> Hiring at AB InBev is very selective. As much as possible, it's internal breeding. That is on purpose. For instance, the last time I recruited in Europe, I screened nine thousand applicants for twenty-five jobs. New people are followed especially closely for the first five to seven years. They are tested right from the start to see if they can thrive in the meritocracy. Everyone talks about it in the company. It is a target system built on aggressive and big targets. People who make it through our process receive opportunities at a young age that you would not get in another company until you had proven yourself five times. We pressure-test the people we hire to make sure they embrace big, risky targets. It is pure meritocracy within the company. If you achieve your targets over time, you will do extremely well financially in our system; the origins go back to the behaviors of the founders that have been passed on.
>
> We treat our people as if they own their part of the business. No delegation or excuses are tolerated. I have worked with our CEO for years. He is the toughest but fairest boss I have ever had. It was extremely difficult sometimes, but I would get instant feedback, totally blunt, and totally transparent. That is how we want everyone to behave. We probably spend as much as one-third of top executive time on selecting, coaching, and developing people. We are at the extreme of believing in

investing this way. We insist that people feel like entrepreneurs and push everything down toward the front line. For instance, we have a company of 155,000 people, yet only about 300 of them are in the corporate headquarters. We have benchmarked against other large consumer companies where there are thousands and thousands in the headquarters. That is not us.

There is no delegation and little tolerance for excuses. You either perform or not; you are paid for solutions, not effort. You are paid to bring proposals, not wait around. People don't write twenty pages of explanation of what happened, but tell it in five minutes and then turn to what you are going to do. Just look at the best neighborhood bakers. They have no one to blame, know the smallest detail of pricing the product, know the customers by name and preference, and feel personally responsible for every detail.

AB InBev's CEO, Carlos Brito, summed things up succinctly for us. "The way we've built our company has always been with this constant dissatisfaction about our results and our achievements," he said. "So we're never happy with where we are. We always think we can do more."

We've observed that kind of thinking time and again in studying scale insurgents and, in doing so, have come up with five important techniques for embedding the owner's mindset in an organization. All business leaders should ask themselves how often and how well they employ them.

- Dream big at every level.
- Unfailingly embrace the principles of meritocracy. Do it openly, without apology. Promote fast, honest feedback.

- Promote from within as much as possible. Ensure that senior leaders invest massively in the people around them.
- Set big but simple targets for the units of value creation in the company, and empower the leaders to act like entrepreneurs.
- Have a zero-base mentality for everything, from yearly budgets to the future of the business model itself.

Liberate Trapped Resources through Zero-Based Budgeting

The CEOs of big companies often complain about the problem of trapped resources. The problem isn't a lack of resources. The companies have plenty. The problem is that most of those resources are locked away in market, product, or functional silos, and seem impossible to redeploy on a moment's notice, even though that's precisely what's required for a company to successfully tackle the dynamic challenges of growth. No matter how hard they try, these CEOs feel they can't create the right culture or incentives to encourage employees to offer up resources to be redeployed elsewhere. This isn't surprising: professionals in bureaucracies get territorial about "their" talent and money, and develop highly sophisticated strategies for defending it. It's the owner's mindset in reverse.

Companies experiencing or aspiring to hypergrowth can't afford to have this happen. So they have to work constantly to simplify and to reinforce transparency. And one of the most effective ways they can do that is by constantly "zero-basing" budgets and the deployment of resources.

What does this mean? Regularly examining every process and every key activity with a fresh eye, and asking these questions: If we could start over, would we still invest here? Is this still the best use of resources, or is it an artifact of history and past budgets? Are our core customers willing to pay for this cost or that process?

These kinds of questions are what AB InBev asks reflexively, almost unconsciously, across the business. At budget time each year, for example, management has to defend and justify every element of its spending. The company eschews perks such as special parking, high-end transportation, and lavish lunches. It does not hold major management meetings at exotic resorts but at AB InBev facilities around the world. This top-to-bottom attention to detail and spending has allowed AB InBev to achieve a level of profit per hectoliter of beer that, according to our calculations, is significantly higher than its global rivals. As a result, AB InBev has grown to be the largest and most profitable beer company in the world. It is, in fact, one of the great insurgents of our time. And here's the thing: despite its boot-camp culture, the company has people beating down its doors to get in. In 2014, it had nearly 100,000 applications for 147 graduate jobs—numbers that top most of the tech firms of Silicon Valley. That's the power of the owner's mindset practiced across an entire company.

These three strategies—building the insurgency, embedding front-line obsession, and demanding an owner's mindset—represent the powerful core traits of the founder's mentality. In this chapter, we've shown how useful they can be in helping insurgents successfully survive overload as they make the journey north. In our next chapter, we'll show how they can help more-mature companies successfully survive stall-out.

USING THE FOUNDER'S MENTALITY IN YOUR ORGANIZATION

✓ Create a forum of franchise players to provide a front-line viewpoint on how to restore the founder's mentality. Give them three immediate tasks:

- Review the agendas of key management meetings during the past six months with the goal of assessing whether the meetings focused enough on customers and front-line employees.
- Identify immediate actions to speed up their ability to serve customers.
- Decide how best to design and test next-generation business models to respond to new insurgents.

✓ Start "Monday meetings" to speed decision making and unblock barriers.

4

Reversing Stall-Out

How to Rediscover What Made You Great When Growth Slows

At some point in their journey, we estimate that two-thirds of maturing companies will find themselves encountering the second predictable crisis of growth: stall-out (see figure 4-1). This is an incredibly frustrating place for leaders because none of the natural sources of propulsion of the past seem to generate the speed and momentum that they once did. The solution, you begin to realize, is to do something different. But what? How much of the solution requires a new outside course of action, a new strategy? How much of the solution requires internal changes, to your crew or even to your ship itself?

Let's begin our discussion by returning to the story of The Home Depot in 2007. We left off with the company in deep trouble, having lost 55 percent of its market value in seven years. Greg Brenneman, the longest-serving member of the company's board of directors,

FIGURE 4-1

Stall-out: The crisis of slowing growth

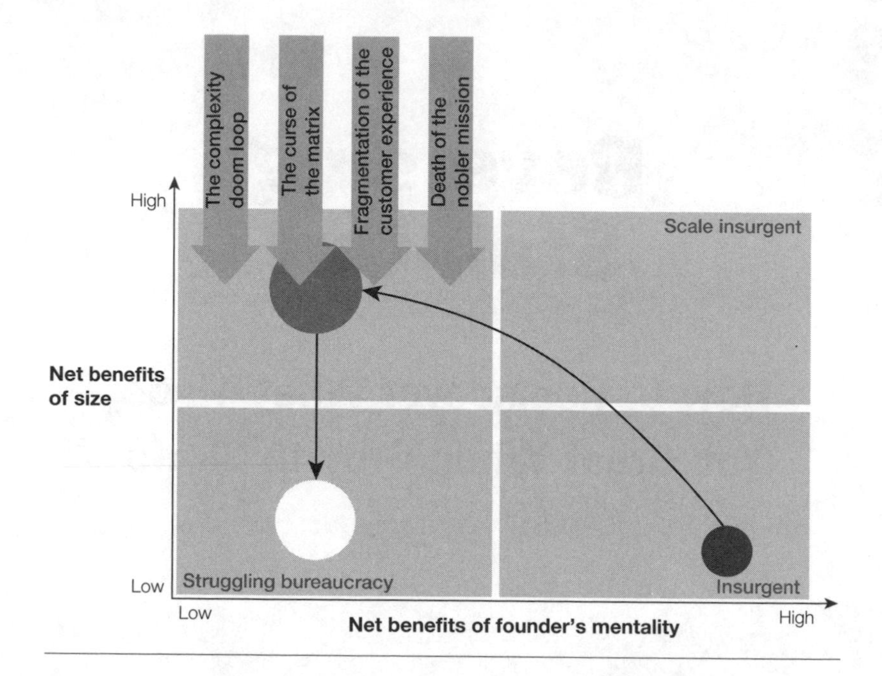

summed up the company's situation for us recently. "A large crack had opened up in its foundation," he told us. "That crack was growing, and the causes were internal and controllable, not external."

Bringing Back the Founder's Mentality

After its controversial CEO Robert Nardelli resigned in 2007, the board elevated Frank Blake to CEO. Blake recognized immediately that he had to deal with the deteriorating customer experience and disempowered employees at the front line that had undermined the company's founder-inspired strengths. He therefore made repersonalizing the front-line experience for customers and employees his top priority.

Right from the start, Blake broadcast one message loud and clear: the founders' mentality was back. On his very first day on the job, he spoke to all employees via The Home Depot's internal television station, during which he quoted extensively from the founders' book, *Built from Scratch*. In particular, he highlighted two of their charts. One highlighted their core values and another gave pride of place at the top of an inverted triangle to the company's front line—its stores where customers and employees interact. Brenneman stressed the importance of this shift in emphasis. "The first thing Frank did," he said, "was to embrace the founders, Bernie Marcus and Arthur Blank. When Frank showed up at the store manager meeting with the legendary Bernie Marcus at his side, everyone knew things were going to change."

Many of Blake's first initiatives focused on reempowering the Orange Apron Cult: the front-line store employees who advised customers. At Marcus's suggestion, Blake also began anonymously visiting store after store on "undercover missions," as he called them. These proved so valuable that he mandated that each of his senior executives work periodically in stores, something most had never done.

Blake then launched a series of coordinated rejuvenation initiatives. He restructured the businesses, closed a series of money-losing stores that had been opened as the crisis unfolded, sold The Home Depot supply business, and shut down another business of fancy appliances called Home Depot Expo, essentially shrinking to grow and to focus on the core stores. Blake also set in motion a massive overhaul of the company's supply chain, creating a network of nineteen regional distribution centers to reduce out-of-stocks and simplify the inventory task at the stores—a move designed to allow store employees to focus more time again on customer service. He also increased the employee bonus pool by a factor of six, rehired some veterans, and asked store managers to return to the

FIGURE 4-2

Stall-out and recovery of The Home Depot

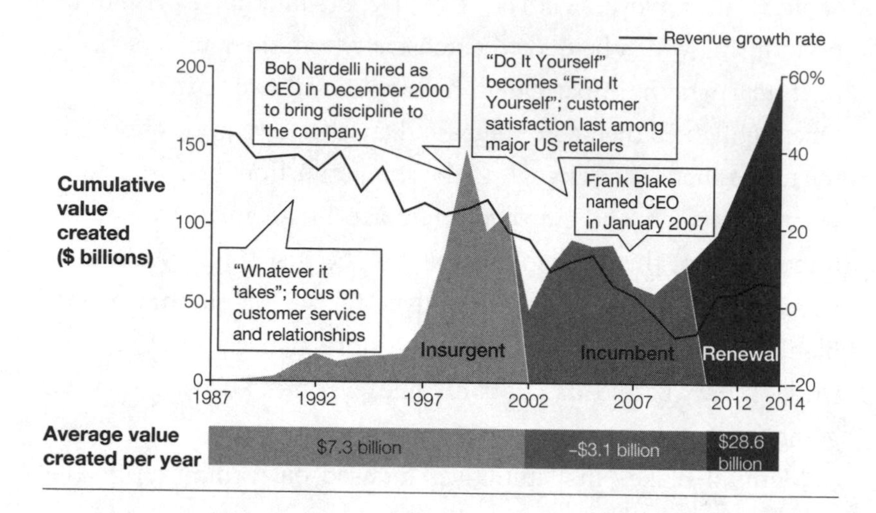

pre-Nardelli policy of giving out honor badges to employees who have been exceptionally attentive to customers.

Eight years ago, The Home Depot had stalled out and was facing the prospect of free fall. But today, thanks to Blake's renewal of the founder's mentality, the company has reenergized its employees and repersonalized its customer experience, an effective return to core principles that has made the company's stock hot once again. It has risen from about $20 per share to more than $120 (see figure 4-2).

The Importance of the Inner Game of Strategy

Large-company stall-outs like that of The Home Depot are surprisingly common. The odds are that during the next fifteen years, two out of every three of the world's multibillion-dollar companies will either stall out, go bankrupt, be acquired, or break into pieces.

Furthermore, the success rate of renewal for those who stall out is small, less than one in seven (see figure 4-3, which is based on tracking the performance of the *Fortune* 500 from 1998 to 2013). These findings parallel those reported by others, such as the Corporate Executive Board, which looked at the 500 largest public companies for a fifty-year period from 1955 to 2005. The cost of stall-out translates quickly into economics; for instance, nearly nine in ten stall-out companies will lose over half of their market value.[1] Just imagine the ripple effects of this on the value of employee retirement plans, investor returns, and the career outlook of the most talented people.

Those companies that recovered generally did so by narrowing, simplifying, and rebuilding the core business, and renewing characteristics the company had when it was at its best. In over two-thirds of the stall-outs, the problem was not related to the emergence of a

FIGURE 4-3

Frequency of stall-out and recovery

***Fortune* 500 companies**
(Review period 1998–2013)

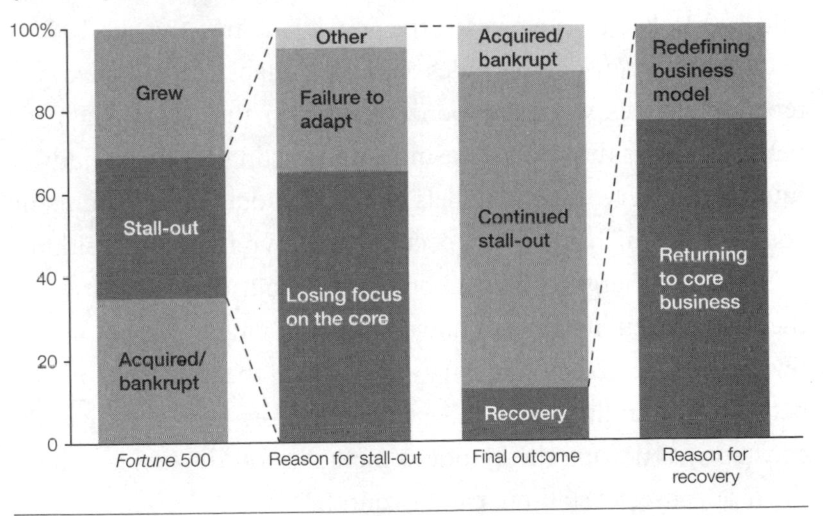

new business model that had burst onto the scene, as Amazon did to the traditional book sellers, or as Uber is trying to do to traditional taxi services. Nor was it that a huge new technology led to tectonic shifts in the industry rules of the game, as mobile phones are doing in markets like retail payments. Usually the problem was internal.

Complexity is the single most common cause of stall-out. This is a growing problem for incumbents, because fast young insurgents are acquiring market power faster than ever before. Well over half of executives now believe that their main competitor in the future will be a different company than the one they are competing with today—one that is simpler, younger, faster, and armed with fresh new technology. This reminds us of what the historian Niall Ferguson has written about the dissolution of empires that once seemed permanent and all-powerful. "When things go wrong in a complex system," Ferguson has written, "the scale of disruption is nearly impossible to anticipate." Entire economies, Ferguson has found, "move from stability to instability quite suddenly," and as proof he cites the astonishingly rapid collapse of empire after empire (France in the 1700s, four years; the Ottoman Empire in the early 1900s, five years; the British Empire in the mid-1900s, less than ten years; the Soviet Union in the late 1900s, five years). Ferguson concludes that the collapse of complex systems accelerates when component parts on the inside begin to behave in ways that are increasingly uncoordinated and at odds, a finding that very neatly parallels our own about large, incumbent companies, which, of course, occupy their own imperial position.[2]

So how do large, complex companies avoid this fate? How do they keep their insurgency alive while moving from being the revolutionary in their industry, or at least the upstart, to now becoming an industry incumbent, if not its key representative? By constantly renewing the founder's mentality on the inside, where the root causes of stall-out can be found.

When we examine the targeted actions that leaders have taken to reverse or prevent incipient stall-out, we find that they often involve a renewal of the founder's mentality, usually with a primary focus on one element rather than all three at the same time. This is different from free fall, which we'll cover in the next chapter, where all elements usually need to be attacked at once, under emergency conditions.

Reigniting the Insurgency

Companies in incredibly dynamic markets sometimes face stall-out because they have grown in complexity, slowed down, and lost a clear sense of their business insurgency along the way. Humans have difficulty keeping complexity under control; it is why our houses are filled with things we no longer need, and why calendars get filled with extraneous activities. Companies, especially those in dynamic industries, have the same problems. Projects, assets, activities, businesses, and processes accumulate but are seldom shed. The result is a loss of focus, a loss of energy, and a dilution of the clarity of what is really important. As counterintuitive as it might sound, the best way to renew focus and rekindle the sense of insurgency is not by starting with a newly crafted mission, but to first take bold action to liberate resources, to demonstrate commitment, and to narrow focus. Then you can use these resources to make your renewed mission real.

Launch an Assault on Complexity and Its Costs

Before doing anything else, a stalled-out incumbent should first simplify its portfolio, free up resources, and begin shutting down noncore projects. When we studied ten successful rescue-and-rebirth operations that we helped clients to engineer, we found that *all* of them involved reducing operating cost by at least 8 percent, and sometimes more than 25 percent. That sort of dramatic reduction of complexity does more than just improve financials and streamline operations. It also liberates resources that make it possible to fund a genuine transformation and to acquire business-redefining capabilities, both of which help incumbents prepare to confront new, insurgent competitors.

More broadly, we've learned through years of experience that the best way to attack complexity is from the top down. This requires several steps. First, you have to shed noncore assets and businesses in a portfolio. Then you have to develop a simpler strategy for the remaining businesses. Then you have to attack the complexity of the organization and the core processes. And finally you have to go after complexity in product offerings, suppliers, and product design. We've seen teams attempt transformation in the reverse order, only to get trapped in the weeds before getting to what really drives most transformations: the reduction of high-level complexity and cost, in concert with a renewal of the insurgency across the company.

For a sense of just how effective this approach can be, let's consider the case of Cisco.

Few companies epitomize the rise of the Internet and Silicon Valley better than Cisco. Founded in 1984 by Leonard Bosack and Sandra Lerner, a husband-and-wife team working at Stanford University, the company became the first to market a router that let different computers communicate smoothly—the key to the World Wide Web and the Internet as we use them today. Cisco routers and switches became the industry standard, capturing and holding about 60 percent of the global market for an amazing three decades. The company, run since 1995 by John Chambers, grew at over 27 percent a year between 1995 and 2005, during which time its market value rose to over $550 billion, making it the most valuable company on the planet. Cisco literally powered through the crisis of overload without a hitch, growing a massive company, retaining its business position leadership, professionalizing management and its systems, and becoming the clear incumbent for well over a decade.

But, as is true in most technology markets, things have changed quickly. New founder-led companies—Huawei, Juniper Networks, Arista Networks—have emerged, and they are fast, focused, and flexible. Cheaper hardware and more-sophisticated software are now available, shifting the profit pool to new skills, equipment, and software. Mobile technologies are changing the nature of the game, too. As a result, since 2005, Cisco's growth rate has dropped to 7 percent. Concerned, investors have steadily pushed the market value of the company down, and today it stands at about $140 billion, less than a third of its peak. Cisco's former chief operating officer, Gary Moore, recently described the situation the company was confronting then:

> Though we were highly profitable and still growing, we had some burning platforms inside and outside the company that motivated the transformation. Externally, our growth was slowing, falling short of our targets, and creating a decline in stock price that, if not stemmed, would have driven the public value of the company below its cash value.
>
> In addition, because our investment portfolio had grown so complex, we were underfunding some key projects in our core business in order to fuel the growth of the fifty-six adjacencies we had moved into, like Flip Video, which we eventually exited. Though we were spending over $5 billion in R&D (over 10 percent of sales), it was not managed as a portfolio of bets. To make matters worse, we were making

> decisions in large boards and committees we called councils, often with no decision power to rationalize these initiatives. In fact, the past growth strategy had drawn so much energy into the many new adjacencies that some of the best engineers did not feel that the core business, the source of most of our cash flow, offered a great future, sometimes causing them to leave. It is one reason that [Silicon] Valley is filled with great Cisco engineers who left: we were not investing enough in the core of the company. Everyone was pursuing "bright shiny objects." Customers were giving us feedback that we needed to be more responsive relative to competition, too. Though we were still a strong leader in our core, the internal and external indicators were crying out that we had to do something.

And so Moore and his team did. They simplified processes, identified noncore businesses and assets to shed, and zero-based their expense budgets, all as part of a program called ACT, short for Accelerated Cisco Transformation, which they insisted quickly become self-funding. Its goals? "Simplify, empower, and increase accountability"—goals not unlike the ones embodied in the founder's mentality.

Here's how they got things going. First, they created eight different initiatives focused on simplification, cost reduction, and speed, with a senior executive in charge of each. They reached out to the key players in their business at all levels—front-line salespeople, engineers, suppliers, and partners, along with leading-edge customers—and collected their diagnoses of the situation and ideas for improvement. These conversations are ongoing. In recent years, as Cisco has found itself increasingly under threat from fast, insurgent attackers, the conversations have focused on the best ways to reduce the cycle time for new products. Through the ACT program, which has emphasized the importance of connections between management and key players at the front line, the company has reengineered its product-development process, created new project-management software, and hired engineers with expertise in methods of fast cycle times. And it's working: after implementing these plans, Moore told us, in some product areas Cisco has taken products that would have taken three to five years to develop and shortened this to eighteen months. Today, the company believes itself to have set the industry standard in this arena.

Since ACT began four years ago, Cisco is faster, leaner, and more focused. Employee- and customer-satisfaction scores are up. The company is 15 percent larger than it was four years ago, but has fewer employees. Its stock price has doubled; its margins have increased by four percentage points, generating nearly $3 billion of profit.

Rediscover the Insurgency of the Past

When companies shrink themselves to regroup, redeploy, and grow, they often rediscover the power of the original insurgency and develop a renewed commitment to pursuing it. That's what happened with Perpetual, Australia's oldest trust company, which achieved rebirth by reducing operating cost by 20 percent and stripping away noncore businesses. The result, one industry observer has noted, was "the largest transformation in Australian financial-services history."

Perpetual was founded in 1886 to manage trust and estate activities for Australia's wealthy elite, and it did this very well, quickly becoming the largest such firm in the country. For more than a century, the company remained the leader in the Australian market, but as it grew, it diversified into eleven new business areas, and by 2011, as it headed toward its 125th anniversary, the company was struggling. Its stock price had fallen from a high of $84 per share to $19—an 80 percent drop in only five years. Profits were down by 75 percent, with no bottom in sight. Shareholders were calling publicly for major overhaul, and the company was on its third CEO in twelve months, Geoff Lloyd.

Lloyd was deeply concerned at the state of the company when he arrived. He told us:

> I found an organization that was internally competitive and externally cooperative, when it should have been the other way around. We were focused too much on internalizing the reasons we were not growing and assigning blame, instead of being out with clients helping them become more competitive. We had grown incredibly complex over time by entering more businesses, eleven in total, and were not the leader in most of them. We did not seem any longer to have a long-term strategy, and no one could agree on where we wanted to go. The unsuccessful diversifications had caused us to lose our confidence. We were awash in complexity and had become hesitant, internally focused, and uncertain as an organization. That made us slow to decide and slow to react. We had little time to right the ship after such a long period of underperformance. Moreover, there was the additional pressure of private equity firms zeroing in on the company. We had to be transformational and not incremental.

Lloyd undertook some initial fact-finding and concluded that to save Perpetual, he would have to return the company to its core mission, as defined more than a century ago by its founders: the protection of Australia's wealth. To achieve that goal, he realized, he would have to make the company "faster, more confident, and, above all, simpler," and to do *that* he would have to resort to immediate "open-heart surgery."

Lloyd began by replacing ten of the eleven members of the management team with people who did not have a vested interest in the decisions of the past. With his new staff in place, he launched Transformation 2015, a set of five main initiatives overseen by a special program office, designed to bring about radical and swift complexity reduction at all levels. Among them was the "portfolio" initiative, which cut the number of businesses owned by the company from eleven to three (two of the eleven businesses earned about 95 percent of the economic profits), reduced real estate holdings by half, eliminated more than 100 legacy funding structures, and cut back the number of independent business entities by 60 percent. The "operating model" initiative, for its part, reduced the size of the corporate-center staff by more than 50 percent.

As part of Transformation 2015, Lloyd and his team also examined costs across the organization and found that 60 percent of total costs were focused on back-office support, staff functions, and redundant controls and checks. Think about that: the company was putting only 40 percent of its money toward sales, customer service, and investment, even though these were its core activities. Deeper down in the organization, Lloyd and his team found that Perpetual was relying on more than three thousand different computer systems and applications. Not surprisingly, the average company employee was making more than five help-desk calls per month, hardly a sign of efficiency.

Cutting back—on businesses, bureaucracy, staff, costs, computer systems, and more—was central to Lloyd's transformation plan. But, critically, he and his team also focused at the same time on a positive plan to invest and gain market share in the company's core, as when it used resources liberated by internal restructuring to acquire The Trust Company, a move designed to increase market share in its core wealth-management business. The transformation team also worked concertedly to engage employees, especially those at the front line. Lloyd convened many town-hall meetings, something that had never before happened at Perpetual, to discuss the company's situation, its plan forward, and its core values. "We labored over the wording of our mission and strategy," Lloyd told us. "Now people live and breathe our vision, which is to become Australia's largest and most trusted independent wealth manager. We created a strategy on one page that we called One Perpetual, with one simpler set of measures and a focus on transparency. We held people accountable where they were not acting consistently with One Perpetual and our values, and we celebrated leaders who did, changing our compensation system to match."

Collectively, Lloyd's strategies brought about a stunning turnaround. Perpetual's stock price has doubled from its low point, when Lloyd took over; employee engagement has increased from 40 to 60 percent; the company is gaining share in its core markets; and net profits have more than tripled. The lesson in this story is simple but critical: for a company in stall out, the key to rebirth is a radical and swift reduction of complexity and cost throughout the company, in order to renew the insurgency on all three of its dimensions.

Renewing a Front-Line Obsession

Another approach to reversing stall-out is to renew from the front line backward. We found this to be the preferred route in companies where customer intimacy is critical to how the business competes, or where deep front-line engagement is especially important in helping companies constantly improve and adapt. As we noted at the beginning of this chapter, The Home Depot has done this very well. So has the industrial giant 3M.

Rediscover Lost Practices of the Past

Sometimes the founders really did get it right in the first place. That's what Sir George Buckley realized upon taking over 3M in 2005. He had to go back to the future.

At that point, 3M had been a leader in the adhesives-and-abrasives business for more than a century. Thanks to a steady investment in R&D, the company had consistently made innovation one of its core competitive advantages. Post-it Notes, Scotch Brand tape, optical films: these iconic products all emerged from the 3M labs during the company's long incumbency.

By 2005, however, the company had begun to lose its way, its mojo, and even its confidence. Unsure of the continuing growth potential of its longtime abrasives-and-adhesives core, its executives had begun focusing their attention on two of the newer businesses in the portfolio—pharmaceuticals and optical films. In the process, Buckley told us, they had cut core R&D by 20 percent and capital spending by 65 percent. Prices in the core business had declined by 12 percent, and the percentage of new products in development had dropped to its lowest level ever. Employee morale was suffering, especially at the front lines and among the key product developers, who felt increasingly shackled by financial reporting requirements and a loss of flexibility.

Buckley, an Englishman who had spent most of his career running global firms, was brought in to revive the company, and almost immediately he diagnosed its problems as internal. "I found a company that had lost its moxie and its confidence in the core," he told us. "The engineers and R&D people were feeling dejected and rejected. They had been the heroes of 3M but were no longer revered. In fact, they were blamed for the low growth. In the heyday, we had been making 30 percent of our revenues from products newer than five years old, but when I began, we were at only 8 percent. We were playing the cost game, not the innovation-and-differentiation game, which had always been our success. Our core markets were growing at an average of 3.5 percent, yet we were growing in those markets at only 1.5 percent. We were starving the company to death. Essentially, it was coming apart psychologically, operationally, and financially."

Buckley acted quickly to return 3M to its core mission and practices—"to a world where innovation in the core mattered again," as he put it to us. He sold off the pharmaceuticals business and focused on once again empowering the front-line bench engineer. He reopened shuttered labs and reinstated the policy of giving engineers one day per week to work on their own ideas. He encouraged self-organizing forums in which the technical people could discuss new ideas. He attended thousands of meetings, at all levels, and visited hundreds of plants. In everything he did, he strove to embed a sense of internal entrepreneurship, self-belief, and empowerment as deeply as possible in the company.

The results were impressive. By the time Buckley retired from 3M in 2012, he told us the company's employee-engagement and employee-satisfaction numbers had more than doubled; growth in the core had climbed out of negative territory and reached 7 percent; and 34 percent of the company's revenues were once again coming from products less than five years old. At the time of his retirement, Buckley received 3,200 letters from employees thanking him for restoring the elements that had made 3M great. And on his last day, he found more than 1,200 people waiting outside his door to shake his hand, a moving testament to the power of the founder's original insights and, perhaps, also of the founder's mentality in general.

What motivated Buckley more than anything, we sensed in our conversations with him, was a deep, almost spiritual feeling of responsibility for the great engineering legacy at 3M, and especially for the thousands of people working tirelessly in the trenches. These were the people who ultimately made everything possible. Great founders and leaders exude this sense of reverence and responsibility. As Buckley said to us about his time at 3M, and not dissimilar from what we have heard from other leaders, "I was just possessed by some deeper feeling about what was right and what was wrong. My sense of responsibility, looking back, was deep; I had complete devotion to the legacy of this great company."

Recreating the Owner's Mindset

Sometimes, especially in high-touch service businesses and businesses where the key employees are spread across lots of autonomous units, the best approach to begin to attack stall-out is to reempower, reenergize, and refocus the army of people at the front line. Recall the remarkable fact that we cited earlier in the book: that employees who feel engaged and empowered—who possess an owner's mindset, in other words—will volunteer solutions to problems and come up with innovative ideas 3.5 times as often as those who don't.

Reintroducing an owner's mindset is a powerful technique for resisting the southward winds and avoiding stall-out. And there are several ways to do this. One is to foster entrepreneurs within the company itself, changing the mix of leadership, creating new role models, and engineering "mini-founder" experiences that create this sense of ownership. Another is to change the ownership of the company itself. At the extreme, this might involve going private, taking in professional private equity partners, or both.

Let's look at each of these approaches, starting with the idea of going outside of the company to acquire young companies and engaging their founding team productively in the larger enterprise. Many companies, particularly those in technology-driven businesses such as Cisco and eBay, have done this successfully. To illustrate, we turn to the example of eBay.

Go Outside to Renew the Inside

When John Donahoe took over as CEO of eBay, he faced some enormous challenges. Initially a huge success story, and one of the first dot-com companies to scale to a large size, by 2008 eBay had stalled out, a victim of new online retail competitors and of its own attempts at diversification, including the purchase of the telecom company Skype. Its aging e-commerce auction model now seemed vulnerable to competitors, and its stock price was in steep decline, having dropped from $59 per share in 2004 to a low of $10.

Donahoe recognized what was necessary to get the company moving again. He had to divest from the noncore businesses the company had acquired, he had to revamp its e-commerce platform, and, most important, he had to shift its focus to one of the great hotbeds of innovation today: mobile commerce. He knew he needed to make a spiky investment in a new capability, and mobile, he understood, was the place to do it. To successfully enter the mobile space, however, he realized he would have to turbocharge eBay's innovation pipeline and capabilities, and the only way he could manage *that*, he told us, was "to fill eBay with young entrepreneurs." So he began to do just that, guided by what he knew about helping companies in stall-out: to succeed, sometimes you need *to bring in outside forces to help.*

Not long after he took over the helm, Donahoe began to acquire small, founder-led companies at a clip of about one every three months. He was especially interested in keeping these new founders and their teams within the company, often so that he could move them into core-business positions, where they could apply their insurgent skills at scale. "Many of these founders like our approach," Donahoe told us, "because they can innovate at scale in eBay, and they get to expose their innovations to 130 million customers globally."

That's the approach Donahoe adopted with many of the founders he brought into the company, such as the then-twenty-five-year-old Jack Abraham, the founder of Milo.com, a company that searched stores for the best-priced merchandise. One day, at a regular Friday meeting that Donahoe held with company leaders under thirty, Abraham raised his hand and proposed a major innovation for the core business. Donahoe told him to go figure out what he needed to explore the idea. Immediately after the meeting, Abraham found six of the best developers at the company, went out for drinks with them that night, and convinced them to leave with him the next morning for two weeks in Australia to work on developing a prototype.

What they came back with blew Donahoe away. "It was the best innovation I had seen in years," he told us. "Had we asked a normal product team, I would have gotten back hundreds of PowerPoints and a two-year time frame and a budget of $40 million. Yet these guys, with the 'founder's mentality,' as you call it, went away, worked 24/7, and built a prototype. These guys see things most can't see. They build. They do no PowerPoint. They just build."

This strategy—bringing in outside help to revive the owner's mindset—has paid off handsomely for many companies. It has been one element of eBay's turnaround, along with other developments, among them the successful spin-off of PayPal, which has given eBay more independence—another example of how to enhance the founder's mentality. In Donahoe's seven-year tenure as eBay's CEO (before stepping down to serve as the chairman of PayPal), the company's stock price has increased five-fold. Obviously, this approach is most suited to companies in fast-moving markets where incumbents need to constantly add technologies and build new capabilities. But for those companies, it can be a very effective way of creating new entrepreneurial energy.

Sometimes you don't even need to go outside for help. Instead, to dial up the founder's mentality, you can create your own entrepreneurs by fostering new businesses and "mini-founder" experiences. We are *not* talking here about how companies can create the conditions for internal start-ups, a strategy that has been covered extensively in the business literature, and that has been adopted over the long term by a number of big companies with stall-out problems, including General Electric. As we've said, our approach in this book is to focus on solutions that companies can implement more quickly in order to produce meaningful results in the short term. Telenor Group is a case in point.

Create Internal Founders

The Telenor story starts in 2007, when a telecommunications engineer named Ronny Bakke Naevdal arrived at Telenor Pakistan as its new head of strategy. Telenor had grown to become the country's leader in mobile communications—no small feat in a country with one of the highest penetrations in South Asia—but the company lacked the robustness necessary to stay on top in Pakistan's highly complex and costly market. It was lacking in new growth opportunities. Naevdal's mission was to reverse this trend, and not long after he arrived, he and his team decided that the best way to do so would be to develop an entirely new business in mobile banking.

"When we started to really study this in detail in Pakistan," Naevdal told us, "we were struck by a few facts on the ground. First, we were the market leader in mobile subscriptions, had a known and well-trusted brand, and had an amazing geographical footprint, across 150,000 points of sale in small shops throughout the country. Virtually no one else had this kind of scale asset. Surely this could be leveraged somehow. Second, Pakistan had only 4,000 bank branches in this entire country of 180 million people, resulting in less than 40 percent geographical coverage of basic banking. Third, what people were often doing to transfer money was incredibly convoluted. We saw a big opportunity to build a new business to solve this fundamental problem."

Naevdal's goal was basic but ambitious: make mobile transfers standard, simple, blind, and inexpensive. In a large and complex country such as Pakistan, however, changing banking practices was a formidable task, the kind of job that the founders of a solo start-up would have almost no chance of succeeding at. Lacking any banking knowledge, Telenor quickly realized it needed a partner. Rather than selecting a large bank, as many other companies would have done, Telenor made the bold move of partnering with the small but agile Tameer Microfinance Bank. That association provided powerful advantages including large scale, national presence, and an international reputation. And the company was able to use those advantages to convince regulators to allow significant changes to the banking system that enabled more financial inclusion.

Only a company as large, credible, and powerful as Telenor could convince regulators to allow such changes. And only a company such as Telenor could at once leverage its national reputation and its local relationships with the thousands of mom-and-pop stores. At the same time, only a small, nimble, and high-energy start-up, of the sort Naevdal and his team were creating as mini-founders, could create thousands of points of sale in mom-and-pop stores without a single Telenor employee present. And only a start-up of that sort could partner with (and later buy) an indigenous bank with only six hundred employees.

The approach worked. Because it had adapted so well to local conditions, Naevdal's business took off rapidly, and its success soon made Telenor the largest bank in Pakistan, as measured by transaction volume, with 50 percent market share of mobile banking and 10 percent of the total national cash flow moving through its system. Moreover, the company's control of mobile banking helped reduce churn in Telenor's mobile-phone business and expanded its reach to 200,000 mom-and-pop stores throughout the country. And all of this helped make Telenor a more robust incumbent, better able to resist the southward winds.

In this chapter, we've discussed three ways to attack stall-out, each of which involves a renewal of the founder's mentality. The first renews the insurgency and increases the fundamental metabolism of a company by lowering cost and complexity, as in the cases of Perpetual and Cisco. The second reempowers and reinvests in the people and details at the front line of the business, as we saw in the cases of The Home Depot and 3M. The third revives the owner's mindset by creating internal founders or by changing the ownership structure itself. All three are powerful fulcrums for change, but none is enough on its own to cope with the most dangerous crisis of growth: free fall.

USING THE FOUNDER'S MENTALITY IN YOUR ORGANIZATION

✓ Launch a highly visible campaign against bureaucracy in which you:

- Kill at least one nonessential layer, process, or reporting requirement every month for a year.
- Single out as "the new heroes" those who do what it takes to get things done for customers.
- Create a strategy compass with your leadership team. Use it to guide you toward a set of required front-line routines and behaviors that will allow you to beat competitors every day.
- Routinely ask your people if they would recommend that a friend work at your company. Follow up with those who say no. What needs to change to make them say yes?
- Look at the degree to which power has shifted from the franchise players and the front line to corporate staff and functional departments. Use your Monday meetings to take one action a week to empower your franchise players and ensure that key functions support them more effectively.
- Benchmark cost and speed against your most successful insurgent competitors. Make "getting back in shape" your top priority in closing the gap.

5

Stopping Free Fall

Using the Founder's Mentality to Save a Business in Rapid Decline

Unlike stall-out, free fall is an existential problem that demands an immediate and dramatic response. It's brought on by not just the internal winds of crisis but also by storm conditions on the outside that create sudden, violent, and unpredictable turbulence. It's the combination of these internal and external forces that can threaten your very existence (see figure 5-1).

Free fall most often affects maturing incumbents whose business model comes under attack from new insurgents or is rendered obsolete by technological or market changes. In the case of Charles Schwab—whose story we used in chapter 2 to illustrate the problems of free fall—both factors played a role. In 2004 the company was facing enormous external market turbulence, new

FIGURE 5-1

Free fall: Rapid decline as a result of both internal and external factors

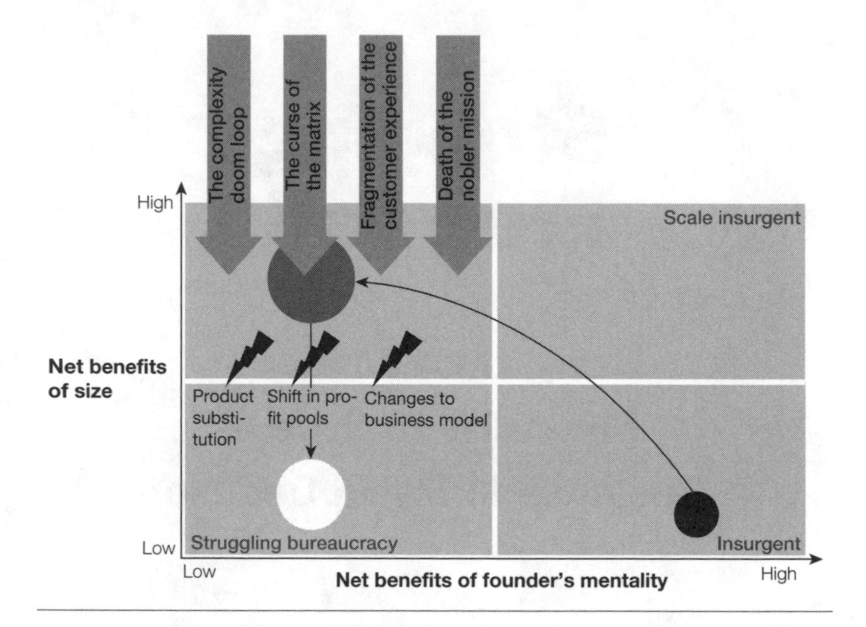

competitors, a 50 percent drop in trading volume, a 75 percent drop in market value, and a reversal of its customer Net Promoter Score from the highest in the industry to the lowest, with 34 percent more detractors than promoters. Internally, there were debates about how much of the trouble was the market and how much was self-induced. But the point is this: when Charles Schwab returned as CEO that year in an effort to save the company, there was not much time left. Things were getting worse fast, and Schwab had to engineer a swift and dramatic transformation.

Charles Goldman, the executive who was put in charge of the transformation, told us how it felt to him at the time. "Chuck wanted to refocus on the client experience," he said. "He turned over half of the executive group right away. Chuck then turned to four areas of focus: renewed value to the customer, improved customer experience, a stronger balance sheet, and the choice of his successor." The first order of business was stabilizing the company financially, lowering cost in order to lower price, and shedding noncore assets and businesses to focus all energy on fixing the original core business. "We did classic reengineering," Goldman said. "We sold all the international businesses, sold the capital markets business we had just bought, simplified corporate service, and downsized the headquarters. We began to move power back to the leaders at the front line with full responsibility, except for shared services that were clearly made subsidiary in terms of decision rights. It used to be that if you sat in an executive committee meeting, the voices that were the loudest were the staff voices. Head of human resources. Head of strategy reporting to the CEO. All these people dominated the meetings, and the business unit heads—the line executives who had the responsibility to actually carry out the strategy and had the most current information from the market—sat there quietly just to get through the meetings. When Chuck returned, we moved it all back the other way."

After Schwab took over, he immediately focused on how dramatically the customer experience had degraded. Originally, it had been one of the company's primary assets. Funding for call centers had been cut in a squeeze for higher margins, and call-center operators were losing energy and confidence. Hidden nuisance and penalty fees to customers had risen to become a significant part of revenue and a significant annoyance to customers. Prices had risen, too, justified by an ever more complex set of products for the eight customer segments the company had set up. One executive told us that customers found the increase in prices particularly galling. "Our competitors were lowering price dramatically to get trades," he said, "sometimes as low as $10. Our headline was $29.95, and the average was $35. Our best customers felt betrayed that we had lost our roots as a discount broker, the original idea of value in the customer experience. This affected the whole orientation of our business toward supporting these fees rather than becoming competitive again."

To pull his company out of free fall, Schwab recognized that he would have to reinvest in the original source of its success and rebuild the company around the essence of what made it once great (its sense of itself as the ultimate insurgent). He understood, for example, that the company's call centers were not a supplementary service that could be squeezed for margins. They were an invaluable tool for developing customer relationships. He and his team quantified the economics of customer loyalty (for instance, many new customers can be traced to positive referrals, which have low sales costs) and put in place a Net Promoter System® so that they could monitor customer loyalty by call center, by employee, by branch, and by team on a daily basis. To reinforce this, they introduced mechanisms and norms for executives to listen to customer calls at the call centers, and to personally follow up with customers who had difficult problems. As for all of those nuisance and penalty fees, Schwab recognized that they represented what our colleague Fred Reichheld calls "bad profits," and since returning, Schwab has eliminated most of them, along with minimum-balance fees. He knew, too, that no turnaround would be possible if he didn't make prices competitive again, so he did, by dismantling the company's complex segmentation and taking massive cost from the company.

His efforts yielded extraordinary success. In just a few years, the company's loyalty scores rose by roughly 70 points, from negative 34 to positive 42. Soon it again had the highest Net Promoter Score in the brokerage industry. The company's stock price soared as a result, quadrupling the company's market value over the next ten years (see figure 5-2).

FIGURE 5-2

The free fall and transformation of Charles Schwab

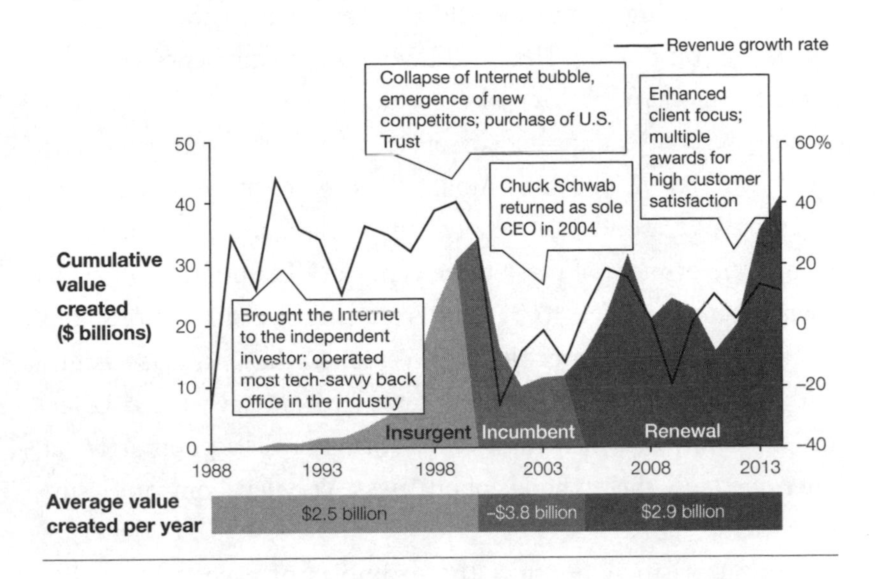

How Free Fall Differs from Stall-Out

We've identified two factors that define free fall and illustrate how it is distinct from stall-out. First, free fall is a time of rapid, almost shocking declines in profitable growth and market value. Think of Schwab's 75 percent decline in value. Second, it's generally triggered by outside market turbulence and the emergence of new competitive business models. This is different from stall-out, where the danger is not yet life threatening and the causes, like complexity, tend to be mostly internal.

In researching this book, we examined a sample of 123 companies, each in a different market, and worked with experts to characterize how many of them were facing major threats of obsolescence in parts of their business model. We identified three forms of disruptive threat in particular. One is product substitution—the shift to smartphones, for example. Another is a major shift in the profit pools, of the sort that energy companies are encountering due to the effect of the smart grid and energy exchanges on pricing. The third involves the emergence of a new business model to deliver the product to consumers, as is happening with streaming video services that are competing with traditional television, or as Amazon did when it disrupted book retailing. We found that 54 percent of companies are currently facing one or more of these three types of disruption to a part of their business model, 16 percent are facing two disruptions, and a few are facing all three threats. We called these threats storms, and categorized them as level one, level two, and level three. Level-three storms, in which these three forms of disruption arrive at once, are truly the typhoons of business. Very few companies survive them.

Not surprisingly, most of the examples of each type of disruption today relate to the Internet and the explosion of digital technologies. Once, these threats of obsolescence were mostly confined to technology businesses, as was the case with Kodak when it faced the digitization of photography. Yet now these disruptions are spreading to even the most traditional sectors. Energy exchanges are collapsing the profit pool of utilities in Europe, Uber is disrupting traditional taxi services, and online degree courses are changing on-campus education.

Unlike stall-out, where one or two focused initiatives can often repel the danger, free fall requires strong, nonincremental action across multiple fronts. When a company is in free fall, the status quo is not an option for those in charge. This is when the number of theories about what to do proliferate. Some will inevitably say, "Just wait; this too will pass." Others will propose jumping into hot new markets, which, our research shows, is almost never the answer. Still others will focus on ways the core business model needs to be redefined. This is a time of loss of consensus, lots of finger-pointing, job risk, and great internal stress.

Although only about 5 to 7 percent of companies experience free fall at any given moment, it is responsible for some of the largest swings in value—both up and down—in the stock market today. (Just think of what happened to Apple, which went down in flames and then rose from the ashes to reach $700 billion in value today.) In the sample of companies we followed that experienced free fall, this period accounted for more than 30 percent of the swings in value. And not only that, free fall is happening increasingly often, now that insurgents are scaling faster, acquiring new customers faster, and capturing market power faster.

We've worked with lots of companies in free fall: our clients at Bain, companies we've been involved with outside of Bain, and even Bain itself, which had a brief flirtation with free fall in the late 1980s. And what we've learned is that reversing free fall requires leveraging the full power of the founder's mentality not just to rejuvenate a company but, in fact, to refound it. We've identified five steps (and one wild card) that have worked in successful turnarounds and transformations.

Essential Steps to Reverse Free Fall by Refounding the Company

1. Build a refounding team.
2. Focus on the "core of the core."
3. Redefine the insurgency.
4. Rebuild the company at the front line.

5. Invest massively in a new capability.
6. Wild card: consider private ownership.

Let's look at them one by one.

Build a New Refounding Team

When we looked at fifty well-documented cases of companies in free fall that turned around their operational performance and transformed their strategic direction at the same time, we found that forty-three of the fifty cases involved massive change in the leadership team, starting with the CEO. The case of Schwab, where over 70 percent of the top-two layers of management was replaced, was typical. In eight of these cases, the founder or the founding family returned to retake the helm, as was the case with Schwab and Apple.

When a company is in free fall, it makes sense to turn over the management team. First, there is the need to inject new energy into a tired organization under stress. The last thing you need is a leadership team that is worn out or not up for the hard work of the transformation. Second, you need to populate the leadership team with people who want to rebuild the future, not defend the past. One executive we interviewed, who was hired in the midst of a transformation, said that when he arrived, "the most common phrase was either 'we used to do it that way,' or 'we don't do it that way here.'" Knowledge of the past is good, but defense of what is no longer working is bad. Rebuilding is hard enough. Third, as the new strategy becomes clear, you may need to add new skills and capabilities, although you should do this with care. You need to hire insurgents with a rebellious spirit—people one executive described to us as "black sheep from blue chips"—rather than employees who are used to the trappings and stability of large companies. This time of transformation can also be a time to find the franchise players who know the detail at the front line and love the company but may not have been promoted to the most visible leadership positions under the past administration. Promoting them is a great sign to the organization, a source of knowledge and energy, and a further signal that the future will be about merit and open-mindedness. Fourth, obviously, it is unreasonable to expect the architects of a strategy and operating practices that led to free fall to see the error of their ways, as well as the right path forward. You want people with open minds to invent the future.

Finally, the change needs to happen relatively quickly. When the majority of a management team is replaced over a long time (tempting because it would seem to reduce disruption), two things happen. First, time is lost. You need to get the team on board before restructuring a business. Second, those who are brought in might begin to absorb the organizational biases of the past.

Focus on the "Core of the Core"

Reversing free fall takes enormous energy and resources. The leaders in most of the successful cases of transformation we've studied knew this and acted on it by combing through the company in search of noncore assets to shed, businesses to sell, activities to stop, functions to eliminate, and product lines to simplify. If the scarcest resource is the time and discretionary energy of the most effective employees, then this is a time to make sure that it is concentrated on the task at hand. One leader told us how the situation on his arrival was like Risk, the board game of international conquest. What he found, he told us, was "a few armies on all sorts of distant territories, and few armies massed on protecting and defending the homeland." He knew what he had to do: "The first order of business was to concentrate forces."

One company that very successfully engineered a transformation along these lines is LEGO. Let's review its story.

LEGO was founded in the 1930s by Ole Kirk Kristiansen, who devoted himself to building a repeatable business model around a system of interlocking plastic bricks. After his death, his successors continued to grow the company, using the repeatable formula, and for many decades during this post-founder phase, the company stuck to its core. By 1993, revenues had risen to $1.3 billion, and in 2000, the LEGO system was voted the toy of the last century by *Fortune* and the British Association of Toy Retailers.

Starting in 1993, however, the company diverted cash from its profitable brick-system business into an astonishing array of adjacencies: theme parks, television programs, watches, retail stores, plastic toys without the brick system, video games, and even a Steven Spielberg co-branded "movie studio in a box." All of these moves drew resources from the core; virtually all of them failed. "As a result," the company's current CEO, Jørgen Vig Knudstorp, told us, "the company entered a ten-year period of declining performance that saw the profit margin go from 15 percent in 1993, to negative 21 percent in 2003. Over this period, LEGO Group lost value at an average rate of 300,000 euros per day." The company was in free fall.

When Knudstorp took over as CEO in 2004, he looked at every option and quickly settled on a course of action. To turn LEGO around and put it on a better path to long-term growth, he decided to return the company to its core and help it rediscover its insurgent mission. He installed a new management team and, with its help, began to strip the business to its basics, focusing the company's energy on rebuilding around the one core product that had made it great: its toy-brick system. His employees embraced the change. "Even though LEGO was in a death spiral," the company's main historian, David Robertson, has written of this period, "many staffers greeted the leadership shake-up with unmitigated joy."[1]

So how did the leadership team at LEGO Group reverse the company's free fall?

First, the team attacked the portfolio of assets. It sold part of the LEGOLAND theme park business to a private equity firm, retaining partial ownership, shut down all of the other adjacencies, and stopped planned expansions: books, plastic watches, LEGO dolls, magazines, the goal of three more theme parks and three hundred more retail stores, software, LEGO Movie Maker, computer games, and even television.

The team then went deeper to further simplify. For instance, it found that the number of unique elements in the LEGO sets had grown massively, from about six thousand in 1997 to more than fourteen thousand in 2004. Colors had proliferated from six to fifty. Moreover, it turned out that 90 percent of these elements were used only one time. So, in addition to cutting businesses, research projects, and toy lines, the team cut all the way down into the components and eliminated more than 50 percent of them. Commenting on this focus, Knudstorp told us, "We are now only investing in products that use repeatable parts and follow repeatable formulas."

From here, the LEGO team began to create rules to determine when products and elements could be added. The cost of a single element is deceptively high, because each requires a separate mold and a machine changeover, and each creates scheduling and inventory complexity on the shop floor. Today, 70 percent of the parts in any LEGO product are from a subset of universal pieces.

The LEGO team then turned to rejuvenate the product line. It built technology into the bricks. It gave online customers the ability to design their own LEGO set or to order the bricks to make structures designed by others. It studied the thousands of the most intense LEGO fans, whose energy and detailed knowledge had never been tapped for conferences, networking events, input into new products, and even active involvement in product design. It began growing again by moving into adjacencies that were tightly linked to the core—LEGO for girls, licensing the brand for a LEGO movie, introducing a new set of mini-figure elements, and increasing the co-branded products, like the *Star Wars* line.

The five steps we listed earlier all played a role in reversing LEGO's free fall. The company changed its management team. It simplified the business on many levels. It redefined the growth strategy around the play system and the user community. Internally, the company renewed its original principles and brought them into a contemporary setting. The designers and key front-line employees again became the heroes of the company. And the company added new capabilities, especially in the digital world. Among the internal moves were some that further symbolized this back-to-basics approach, such as selling off the LEGO Group's headquarters to move into a modest building that also contained the packing plant. The company vigorously committed itself to each step, with amazing results. Since Knudstorp took over, LEGO's revenues have increased by 400 percent, and its operating profit margin has increased from negative 21 percent to positive 34 percent.

This approach—shrinking to grow—has been adopted successfully by a number of companies in free fall. It was true in Lou Gerstner's transformation of IBM: he shed a range of hardware businesses (like PCs) and shifted the company's energy toward services and software. It was true in Steve Jobs's turnaround of Apple: Jobs cut back to four main products and a handful of development projects early in his return as CEO. It was true in the example of Schwab, too, which shed several prominent acquisitions, including U.S. Trust, and reduced significantly the number of different customer segments its salesforce was treating separately. In each case, the approach was the same: first, strip away complexity and, second, return to the core of the core.

Redefine the Insurgency

To reverse free fall requires more than complexity reduction, a new team with the necessary energy and mindset, and liberated resources to fund the transformation. At some point, it is necessary to prove that "there is a *there* there" to justify the work. We have seen many business positions that are so far gone or behind such a large competitive eight ball that the effort is not worth it. To renew the insurgent energy on the inside, the new team will need to prove that it is all worth it on the outside.

Let's look at one company in free fall where this was the central issue. Again, we have chosen an example from a number of years ago in order to see how it played out through the whole sweep of events. Remember, most reversals of free fall ultimately take four to six years because they are so comprehensive in their scope.

In 1994, when (believe it or not) mobile phones had penetrated only about 9 percent of the US market, Ted Miller, an entrepreneur in Texas, had a brilliant idea. Telecom operators, Miller knew, had launched a capital-intensive race to build out the network of cellular relay towers across the world, and he realized that each trying to do this unilaterally made no sense, just as it would have made no sense for car manufacturers to have built their own independent road systems in the early days of the automobile. Miller recognized an opportunity: a savvy businessman could found a very successful business based on the idea of owning and leasing out towers. He ran with the idea, and Crown Castle was born.

Miller started by buying a cluster of 133 towers in southwest Texas and, in 1995, forged an investor relationship with the private equity firms Berkshire Partners and Centennial Funds to help him execute as big a land grab as possible while the industry was still young. The company executed on its plan brilliantly, acquiring towers all over the world and quickly initiating acquisition efforts in more than fifteen different countries. It was an insurgent success story: Miller took the company public in 1998 at a stock price of $13 per share, and by 2000, the price reached $42 per share.

But then investors began scrutinizing the growth model and didn't like what they found: the debt levels, the unending negative cash flow, the uncertain end point of the land-grab strategy. As public confidence in the company evaporated, the stock price fell to $1, driving the company's equity market value below $300 million. Miller stepped down as CEO and left the company soon afterward, and employees marooned at the company found themselves worried about their jobs, their savings, and their direction.

In July 2001, John Kelly stepped in as the company's new CEO and engineered a remarkable turnaround. In a frank discussion, he described to us how he helped the company adapt and restore its insurgent mission.

"The first thing we had to do," he told us, "was to create a common view of our core, our purpose, and of the right way to scale the business. We concluded that it was not a global tower business but a regional-level business, and that we had to focus where we could build systems and services for customers to optimize the economics of each tower. We withdrew initially from ten countries with two more countries ceasing operations shortly thereafter, and focused on building three core markets where we could create regional density and generate market power by becoming the best provider to customers who made tower decisions at that level. The wrong expansion model had led us to taking excess risks outside and underinvesting inside in the systems that would allow us to expand profitably."

Kelly and his team jumped to the forefront of the industry in creating these systems. "We created regional organizations to get more of our people into the field with the customers who made their network decisions on a local basis," he said. "We developed sophisticated models of tower economics and detailed databases of tower attributes to manage the sites. We held meetings and training sessions with each of our employees so that they could understand that our success drivers came from regional density of the network, and deep technical expertise in the eyes of our customers, and how we wanted to grow from that platform. We completely rebuilt the company inside and out."

Redefining the insurgent mission around customer service and leadership in dense regional networks (versus being an acquisition business buying towers everywhere worldwide) drove huge and immediate changes. The company divested towers and countries. It needed to develop new internal systems. It reset the acquisition agenda around local density. And it focused on hiring people who could understand and sell to telecom customers. Without the redefined mission spelled out and understood by the key employees within the first year, the free fall would probably not have been stopped in time. It affected everything, including the hope and energy of those who had to carry it out.

The results have been impressive. Crown Castle's tower count has grown from seven thousand to over forty thousand in little more than a decade, making the company the largest US operator of shared wireless infrastructure. And it has grown in equity market value from about $250 million to over $25 billion.

Crown Castle's redefined insurgency was based on the same market phenomenon that inspired the original insurgency: the knitting together of towers into regional and, ultimately, global networks. Yet its focus, the required skills, and the key profit drivers all changed dramatically. By adding new capabilities, the company changed the business model and, in effect, refounded itself on the fly.

We've found that this approach accounts for about a quarter of the successful cases of free-fall reversal that we studied. But there are other approaches, of course. Apple radically redefined its insurgency and its market advantage at a time when the boundaries of the industry were dissolving, and it needed to acquire or develop the skills to succeed across the range of newly connected markets. Central to Apple's transformation has been its ability to add a series of powerful capabilities inside the company (such as managing online digital content and a new approach to retail stores) as well as outside (Apple's more than three hundred thousand app developers, for instance). These capabilities allowed Apple to fix and redifferentiate its core, while enabling it to move into one new adjacency after another (iPod to iPad to iPhone to Apple Watch) in pursuit of new growth.

Another approach is much more fundamental: some companies focus ruthlessly on strengthening the insurgency and core mission of the past. DaVita, a chain of kidney dialysis centers that went into free fall but then pulled out of it and became the best-performing health-care company of the past decade, is such an example. We'll tell its story in the next section.

Finally, there's what might be called the big-bang approach, which involves transforming a company by having it leap to a new, hot market. Only rarely do companies pull this off. Marvel Entertainment did it, transforming itself from a bankrupt comic-book company to a highly profitable movie company that The Walt Disney Company acquired for $4 billion. Yet even here, Marvel built on its ability to pivot, not leap, into a new market.

Refound the Company on the Inside

A central premise of this book is that the majority of performance problems companies have on the outside actually have a more fundamental root cause on the inside. This premise is important in the case of free fall, because the dynamics on the outside are often so strong that it is easy to stop there. Nokia's free fall, for example, can be attributed to many external forces, among them, Apple's competitive strategy; the problems Nokia had with its mobile operating system, Symbian; and Nokia's few app developers. But the deeper root cause of most of the company's external problems proved to be internal.

One of the most remarkable examples of refounding a company on the inside is the story of how Kent Thiry and team pulled Total Renal Care out of free fall by reinventing it as DaVita.

When Thiry took over as CEO of Total Renal Care in 1999, the company was heading for disaster. Made up of 460 renal-dialysis care centers, it was losing more than $60 million per year, was under investigation by the federal government for fraud, was at risk for failing to meet payroll for its nine thousand employees, and was being sued by shareholders. Patient outcomes were poor relative to industry standards, and the overworked staff, feeling unappreciated and seeing no bright future ahead, was turning over at a rate of 40 percent per year. Reflecting the company's state of crisis, the stock price had collapsed by 95 percent, from $23 per share to $1.71. It is hard to imagine a more disorienting free fall for people inside the company.

Thiry immediately attacked on many fronts at once. He replaced most of the management team, reduced costs to forestall bankruptcy, simplified by reducing the enormous variation in practices across the centers (he told us he found a company of 460 centers doing things in 460 ways), and returned to better customer practices, all of which were necessary simply to stabilize the business and give it some resources to make a turnaround possible. But, critically, he also dedicated himself to a multiyear program of essentially refounding the company from the inside.

To reinforce the idea that everybody at the company had a stake in its rescue and rebirth, Thiry began referring to Total Renal Care as a village. He abolished the use of formal titles internally (though they were still needed externally) and began to refer to himself as a mayor, not CEO. He convened town meetings with local staff and organized national voice-of-the-village phone calls every eight weeks that were often attended by four thousand people from the company's offices or clinics around the country. He asked his employees (internally referred to as "teammates") to come up with a new name for the company and to codify its values, a seven-month exercise that led to the name DaVita (which means "giver of life" in Italian) and seven core DaVita values, among them "one for all and all for one," "continuous improvement," and "service excellence."

Those core values became a critical element of Thiry's transformation plan. He and his team created measures in each of the centers for studying not only how well the center was handling patient care but also how steadfastly its employees were sticking to those values, and they made those measures public and linked pay to them. They began to capture, publicize, and financially reward "DaVita moments" of heroism among front-line employees. They began rating job candidates on how well they seemed to align with the core values. They even brought patients into the process by asking them to vote and comment on the caregivers who most helped them, so that the company could reward them appropriately.

Together, according to Thiry, these changes had two immediate and important effects. First, they helped create a powerful sense of shared mission throughout the company; and second, they had the effect of constantly flattening the organization, drawing the front line closer to the senior management. Increasingly, too, as they created a more repeatable model in the branches, Thiry and his team were able to push more decision authority downward in the organization, leading to a front line that felt more empowered and energized. Thiry realized that senior management needed to be a part of that process and so insisted that each manager spend a week each year working in the centers.

When we first wrote about the DaVita story in 2010, the company had just achieved a remarkable eleven-year run, during which it had become the best-performing stock in the Standard & Poor's 500, earning investors a return of twenty-nine times. From the start of the turnaround to 2010, the company grew its revenues from $1.3 billion to $6.2 billion, and its operating earnings from a large loss to $1 billion. And the growth continues apace. By the end of 2014, DaVita had again doubled in size, to $12.8 billion, and its stock price had risen from $30 per share in 2010 to $84 in 2015 (see figure 5-3).

Thiry obviously employed a variety of strategies to engineer the rebirth of DaVita. But everybody involved will tell you that the internal transformation in values, principles, energy, and behaviors that he engineered was the primary reason for the company's renewal. Today, if you walk through the new DaVita headquarters

FIGURE 5-3

Performance of the refounded DaVita

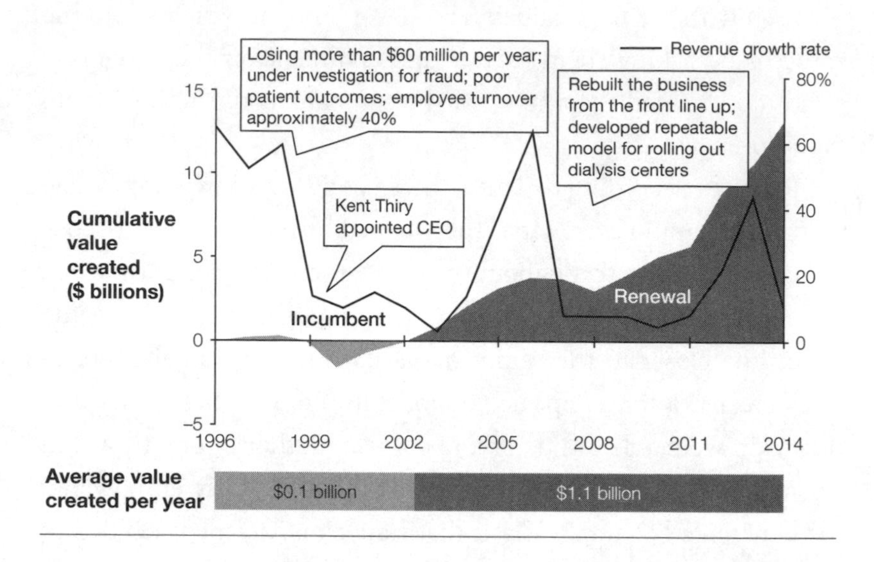

in Denver, Colorado, you'll find cultural iconography everywhere: the seven values of DaVita, photos of the centers and their teams, quotes and sayings that were made meaningful during the turnaround, testimonials from patients praising the work, and hero stories of front-line employees. One big message comes across loud and clear: even when things look dire for a business, renewal might still be possible. But if you go for it, go all out. Refound the company. Don't hold back.

Invest Massively in a Core Capability

Companies in free fall have a lot to fix but seldom have all of the tools they need. They usually find that they are missing at least one capability crucial for adapting their business model to new conditions.

Nearly all of the fifty cases of successful reversal of free fall that we studied required at least one major new capability. For instance, Steve Jobs would not have been able to renew Apple if the company had not built capabilities in digital rights management and retailing, both online and offline. Lou Gerstner would not have been able to renew IBM without building new capabilities in software, consulting, and IT services. John Kelly would not have been able to renew Crown Castle if the company had not built up technical-sales and service capabilities for telco operators to a high level. Reed Hastings would not have been able to renew Netflix had the company not developed the best digital-streaming capabilities in the industry, and the capability, through partnerships, to generate fresh content like the award-winning show *House of Cards*.

A lot has been written about the failure of Kodak, once the world leader in film and photography: how internal breakdowns prevented it from embracing the shift to digital, and how the large film profit pool, which Kodak dominated (accounting at one point for 90 percent of film and 85 percent of camera sales in the United States) encouraged the company to fight the future rather than reinventing it.

Yet some film and photography companies did make the shift and avoid or reverse free fall. For instance, Fujifilm, which was number two globally in film, added capabilities, shifted aggressively to digital photography, restructured to cut complexity and costs, and today is thriving. The company also invested $4 billion in adapting its technology to make optical films for LCD flat-panel screens.

In the photography industry, Leica provides an even sharper example of how adding new capabilities can help a company reverse free fall. The first Leica camera was invented by Oskar Barnack, an engineer who worked for the lens company Leitz.

Barnack succeeded at creating the first lightweight camera whose most distinctive feature was the quality of its lens, allowing small film images to be blown up without losing much resolution. Leica's image quality made it the preferred camera of the great photographers of the last century, among them Robert Capa, the war photographer who captured the D-Day landing; and Henri Cartier-Bresson, who became enraptured by the new camera and its remarkable images. ("The Leica," he said, "feels like a big warm kiss, like a shot from a revolver, like the psychoanalyst's couch.")

Yet the company was slow to embrace digital photography. It invented autofocus but never exploited it in its cameras, and only began to put digital technology into its cameras in 2006. The company's problems were compounded by the decline of traditional photo stores and the rise of the Internet and discount camera retailers. Because Leica made cameras at the top end of the price range and didn't adapt to these changes, it lost money throughout the 1990s. Between 2005 and 2007, Leica saw its revenues decline from 144 million to 90 million euros, and it lost 10 to 20 million euros per year, which made it hard for the company to invest in the new capabilities it needed to compete. The company had entered free fall.

Enter Andreas Kaufmann, an Austrian investor who acquired a controlling stake in Leica in 2006 and believed that Leica possessed unique assets that it could build upon to renew itself—its brand, its unparalleled image quality, its heritage with the great photographers, the quality of its lenses. Kaufmann proceeded to engineer a turnaround of the company focusing on the top end of the market. Then, in 2011, the private equity firm Blackstone invested 160 million euros in the company. This capital, plus Kaufmann's dream to renew Leica, has allowed the company to obtain the new capabilities that were central to revamping its product line (autofocus, digital version of the M line of cameras) and its channels of distribution (branded stores). Today, Leica's revenues have tripled from its low point, and it is again solidly profitable. What the future holds is uncertain, with the wave of smartphone cameras eroding the market for traditional cameras. But for now one of the great brands in photography has reversed free fall and returned as the standard bearer of image quality, just in time for the company's hundredth anniversary.

A leadership team confronting free fall usually feels stretched to the limit. It's hard to think about new capabilities in this state. But if you don't, all of the other work you do to pull your company out of free fall could go for naught. This is a special challenge for leaders. We will return to this topic—the leader's role in building capabilities—in the next chapter.

Wild Card: Return to Private Ownership

Changing the mix of investors to avoid free fall is an option that a growing minority of companies pursue today, a process enabled by the massive growth in private equity firms during the past few decades. Shifting to private ownership can buy time, create currency to attract talent, and reduce external distractions to focus on the difficult internal task at hand.

It worked for the money-losing semiconductor division of Philips, which had roots that traced back to Fairchild Semiconductor, the earliest of all Silicon Valley tech companies. In 2006, the division was sold to a consortium of private equity investors that included KKR and Bain Capital, which promptly named the company NXP, shorthand for "next experience."

It certainly was that. At the time of sale, the industry was in a slide, revenues were in decline, and profit margins were negative

12 percent, trending to bottom out at negative 40 percent. The company was in free fall.

Over the next five years, however, NXP underwent a complete transformation on pretty much every one of our six steps, including moving into private hands for the period of renewal. NXP replaced much of the management team, including the CEO. It simplified the portfolio of businesses and products and much more tightly circumscribed the core business. It divested several businesses, which helped the company shrink from about $6 billion in revenues in 2006 to $3.8 billion by 2009. The organization as a whole was simplified aggressively. It reduced layers of management and staff, taking out a quarter of the total cost base, and developed a more focused strategy to rebuild global market position in the company's most iconic product area of high performance: mixed-signal electronics.

It's been a great success. Since NXP returned to public ownership through an IPO in 2010, it has grown revenues by 30 percent, attained over $1 billion in operating income, and initiated a merger that will double the size of the company. In the five years since its IPO, NXP's stock price has increased tenfold.

When we asked one of the senior executives at NXP about this remarkable story, he emphasized that it would not have happened if the company had remained a noncore business buried within an enormous, publicly traded conglomerate that itself was struggling with its own identity and performance. Furthermore, private ownership made it possible for the company to transform itself away from the scrutiny of stock market analysts, and to focus on four-year rather than quarterly results, the long-term perspective that is at the heart of the founder's mentality.

We are hearing this more and more. Companies in free fall are turning increasingly to private investors for temporary shelter to restructure during free fall or to restore the founder's mentality for the longer term. This is what Michael Dell recently did, in one of the largest public-to-private shifts in history. Though not in free fall, Dell faced stall-out and needed to make a lot of changes, internally and externally, given the rapid and disruptive changes in the computer industry.

Dell's initial story is a remarkable and justly famous one. Few companies have scaled as fast and as profitably in the history of business. Since its founding in 1984 in Michael Dell's dorm room, Dell set the world record for the most-rapid growth in its first twenty years of life—eight times as fast as Walmart and four times as fast as Microsoft. During the 1990s, a period of true hypergrowth (during which Dell made it through overload magnificently without missing a beat), it achieved annual returns to shareholders of an astonishing 95 percent, growing its earnings over this period by 63 percent per year. At its core was its "direct model" for selling computers, which bypassed retailers and had a negative cash-conversion cycle (meaning the company was paid for the computers before paying for all the components). The model at the time advantageously provided customer intimacy (customers ordered directly) and low cost (it had about a 15 percent cost advantage in personal computers over such rivals as Compaq and Hewlett-Packard).

Yet as Dell entered its third decade, a range of developments intervened to drive down its annual growth rate. From 1992 to 1999, growth increased at a remarkable 54 percent per year; from 1999 to 2006, growth declined to 17 percent per year; and by the period 2006–2013, stall-out was imminent. The annual growth rate during those seven years was a mere 2 percent. Many things occurred during this time to bring the highest flyer of all time down to earth. Priorities under new, professional management shifted the focus more and more to cost reduction instead of investing in customers. As a result, Dell's Net Promoter Score went from best to near worst in the industry. New products were also not as "hot" as they were during the growth years when Michael

Dell was at the helm as CEO. Also, the cost advantage of the direct model was declining. The result of all this was impending stall-out, signaled by a 74 percent loss in market value from $94 billion in 1999 to just $26 billion in 2013.

What went wrong? "We took our eye off of the customer," Michael Dell told us recently. Increasingly, as a large public company, Dell had stopped investing in customers and, instead, was devoting its resources to cost reduction and hitting annual market-based benchmarks. By 2014, after failing to turn his company around with incremental measures, Dell decided to adopt a radical approach: he would take Dell private, with the equity partner Silver Lake.

It was an inspired move. "In going private," he told us, "it's amazing how we have been able to speed things up within the company. We simplified meeting structures, went to a board of directors with just three members, and increased our appetite for risk. When big committees talk about risk, they talk about risk committees, how risk is bad, the mitigation procedures of risk, and the reaction of the analysts. Yet now for us risk is about innovation and success. It has been very energizing to our one hundred thousand employees to feel the long-term focus coming back into the company."

Dell has its owner's mindset back, and it's already performing better. Its customer-satisfaction scores have rebounded, and its employee-satisfaction scores are the highest in the company's history. The company's core businesses are outgrowing their industry again, and the company is investing heavily to redefine its model for the long term. "We changed our focus," Dell told us, "to cash flow from quarterly earnings, to the long term from the shorter term, and to investing heavily in new capabilities. It has caused us all to think about the business totally differently."

We recently asked Dell to reflect on this bold move. "We are in a 'change or die' kind of business that has to continually evolve," he reminded us. "To do this, we realized that we needed to build a series of major capabilities for the long term, as well as to invest heavily in customer service. We tried to do this from 2007 to 2013, including a series of acquisitions, but the market was not patient enough. They said, 'Just give us more dividends and repurchase shares.' This is a depressing loop for anyone. We were spending nearly $2 billion per year as it was on dividends, interest costs, and share repurchases. We decided it was time to do something different and change our horizons by going private. Today our horizons are not quarterly, but are three, five, and ten years out in terms of our three priorities: sales capacity, new product, and capability." In fact, as we write this, Dell has just announced the third-largest technology acquisition in history—the purchase of data storage leader EMC, for $65 billion.

Going private is not for everybody, of course, but there is an increasing body of evidence to suggest that returns are higher in private than public hands. We believe strongly that the main reason is the power of the three elements of the owner's mindset—a bias to speed of decision and risk taking, a deeper sense of accountability, and a focus on cash flow. The early returns from Dell, which avoided free fall by going private, add to this weight of evidence.

Nothing about free fall is easy. But it can represent real opportunity. As we've noted, we've found that some of the largest positive swings in value can occur as companies recover from free fall, restore the founder's mentality, and get themselves back on the path to scale insurgency. Sometimes the hardest materials are forged in the hottest crucibles.

In our next chapter, we'll provide specific advice for leaders trying to grow their companies and make them "scale insurgents"—which is to say, companies that achieve sustained profitable growth at scale while also maintaining the strengths of the founder's mentality.

USING THE FOUNDER'S MENTALITY IN YOUR ORGANIZATION

✓ Take immediate actions to ensure your business can survive industry turbulence and respond to new insurgents. Specifically:

- Make the case for change with your people. Are parts of your business model becoming obsolete? If so, focus urgently on how they should be redesigned.
- Radically reduce complexity to liberate resources and sharpen focus, even if this means shrinking the business back to the "core of the core." Demonstrate how actions to reduce complexity and costs create funds to invest in growth.
- Involve your strongest, next-generation franchise players in identifying how the core business needs to change to compete. Ask them for personal commitments to stay and execute their vision.
- Set up a program office of leaders assigned full-time to manage the turnaround and transformation of the business model.
- Ensure that 50 percent of management discussions are focused on investing in capabilities to grow over the long term.

✓ Consider the role of private equity investors or private ownership.

6

Action Plan for Leaders

Infusing the Founder's Mentality at All Levels of Your Organization

We return to our starting premise. To win consistently on the outside in business, you must also be set up to win on the inside. And the best way to do that is to embrace the founder's mentality.

This is the job of the leader, as we've tried to make clear throughout this book, but by "leader" we don't just mean the CEO. We mean all leaders. Imagine the power of an organization in which leaders at every level embraced the founder's mentality. A company of insurgents is a powerful thing. It's what Michael Dell had in mind when, in talking about reviving Dell, he said, "I want to create the conditions of the largest start-up in the world."

This last chapter offers lessons for leaders at all levels in an organization—practical lessons about how to overcome the predictable crises of growth and how to get started on Monday morning.

We bring several strong biases to this discussion.

First, *leadership is learnable*. It can be mentored, measured, practiced, and improved.

Second, *leadership is not just for the CEO*. The companies that most successfully maintain the founder's mentality behave as if they have an army of leaders, not one. The CEO of these companies leads by making his or her people better, as Sir George Buckley did with the engineering leaders at 3M, as John Donahoe did by dialing up the entrepreneurial culture at eBay, and as Carlos Brito has done at AB InBev by giving young, hungry employees large goals and lots of running room.

Third, *the founder's mentality is not just a luxury for companies that are already successful and now want to pay attention to their people*. No, just the opposite. Companies that lose the hearts and minds of their employees, no matter what their size or type of business, will eventually lose to insurgent companies who attack them. Without the founder's mentality, incumbents become bureaucrats, making them increasingly vulnerable to insurgents who are adapting and scaling faster than ever.

Finally, *the attributes of scale insurgents are relevant for all business leaders*. As we've emphasized throughout this book, scale insurgency should be the goal for businesses who hope to grow sustainably and profitably (see figure 6-1). Scale insurgents achieve an advantage from growing to large size (economies of scale, market power, and advantaged learning) *and* from maintaining the traits of the founder's mentality (insurgency, front-line obsession, owner's mindset). And that advantage is hugely significant: scale insurgents account for about two in three companies that

FIGURE 6-1

Scale insurgency as an objective for leaders

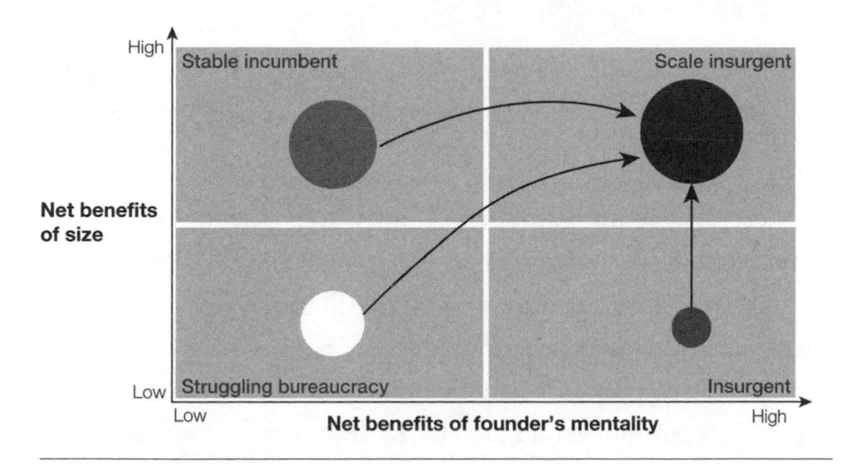

achieve more than a decade of sustained and profitable growth. They also dominate the list of "best places for talent" in their respective industry.

This book is replete with examples of businesses renewed by leaders who saw potential that proved unattainable to their predecessors, and who harnessed the power of the founder's mentality to achieve it:

- Kent Thiry and his team transformed DaVita from a decaying business near bankruptcy to the best-performing health-care company in America.
- Jørgen Vig Knudstorp took LEGO Group back to its core, creating more customer intimacy by transforming it with new technology and new ideas.
- The investors in NXP purchased a company whose parent had given up on it and then renewed it dramatically by simplifying it.

- Motivated by the power of an idea, the founders of AB InBev made an almost profitless Brazilian brewery into one of the great scale insurgents of our time.
- And Steve Jobs, of course, saw potential in Apple when others did not, and made it into the most valuable company in the world.

These leadership teams would all readily cite the many fortunate events that have helped them along their paths to scale insurgency. However, they weren't just lucky. They all believed passionately that they had more potential than most observers recognized. They pursued their full potential relentlessly. As Brito, the CEO of AB InBev, told us, "We're never happy with where we are. We always think we can do more."

Our previous books on strategy have all made the search for full potential their point of departure: full potential in the core (*Profit from the Core*), full potential in surrounding adjacencies (*Beyond the Core*), full potential in businesses whose models are becoming obsolete but still have assets to build on (*Unstoppable*), and full potential in the adaptable, repeatable business model (*Repeatability*). At one level, this book is no different. It, too, makes the search for full potential its starting point. But the difference, as we've pointed out repeatedly, is that all of our previous books focused on the external game of strategy, and this one focuses on the internal game.

That's a game that all leaders have to play well, and we've found that nothing teaches it better than lessons derived from the founder's mentality. We've identified three important areas in which the founder's mentality can teach leaders valuable lessons. Let's explore them next.

Self-Awareness

Companies find it enormously difficult to maintain self-awareness as the crises of growth hit and to make a realistic assessment of their vulnerabilities. To maintain self-awareness, watch out for the following problems:

Fundamental measures are missing. Companies assess their health on the outside with lots of outcome measures (profit, revenues, customer counts, market share, average prices, and so on), but they don't take good stock of the health of the core with nonfinancial, root-cause measures. These are essential. Such measures helped Dell set the world record for speed to scale. We like the idea of using customer and employee advocacy among these measures.

Listening to the wrong voices. What you hear depends on whom you listen to. Leaders who are strapped to their desks and surrounded by staff people who echo their ideas can easily fall into this trap. They have no connection to the fresh intelligence and dissenting ideas that arise at the front line. Consider the case of Ed Telling, the former CEO of Sears, Roebuck & Company, whose story Bernie Marcus, one of the founder's of The Home Depot, holds up as a *bad* example and a motivator to all Home Depot executives. "Telling hated being in the stores," Marcus and his cofounder Arthur Blank wrote, "and that was where the bread and butter was coming from. That was what paid his salary. He never understood that. In this company we do understand that. That is why we insist that every executive of this company works in the stores upon joining us. This policy even applies to our attorneys."[1] It's obviously ironic that this is one of the principles that The Home Depot lost sight of when its founders left. It shows how easily it can happen.

The lesson for leaders: make sure you have access to voices from the front line. They are your best defense against self-deception. Get out to the front line, hold meetings in plants and warehouses, and insist that those reporting to you do the same thing. Well into his nineties, M. S. Oberoi was still commenting on customer cards. Jeff Bezos has a designated person at key meetings to represent the customer voice at Amazon. Kent Thiry of DaVita does weekly calls where any employee can phone in; the last one involved four thousand people. "The bigger Walmart gets," Sam Walton said, "the more essential it is that we think small. Because that's exactly how we have become a huge corporation—by not acting as one."[2] Ray Kroc, the founder of McDonald's, had a great perspective on the power of a bottom-up perspective. "I work from the part to the whole," he said, "and I don't move on to the large-scale ideas until I have perfected the small details."[3]

The tyranny of the short term. The way to lead is not to wait for crisis and then take action. Great leaders manage their time like a strategic resource, both to model the behavior for others and to shift attention to the things that matter most. "If you're in a leadership position," Andy Grove, the founder of Intel, once said, "how you spend your time has enormous symbolic value. It will communicate what's important or what isn't far more powerfully than all the speeches you can give."[4]

Strategic change doesn't just start at the top. It starts with your calendar. Ask yourself whether you are really in control of your own time, and when was the last time you and your team looked at how you spend your time (with customers, in front-line facilities, with high-potential young leaders). The answers might surprise you.

One more tool of self-awareness: use the founder's mentalit and a founder's mentality survey to define your current sitı You can find a simple version of this tool for your use at our website. www.foundersmentality.com. If you don't know where you are in the present, it is hard to figure out the best route to the future.

Common Ambition

"If you don't have a dream," Les Wexner told us, "then it can't come true."

This idea seems obvious, but it can get lost. As companies grow and professionalize, their stated missions can devolve into generic, uninspirational statements of corporate ambition. Barnes & Noble: "to operate the best specialty retail business in America, regardless of the product we sell." Avon: "to be the company that best understands and satisfies the product, services, and self-fulfillment needs of women globally." Too often, mission statements leave employees with no clear idea of what their company strategy is, or what makes it special.

Three bad things happen when an organization's ambition becomes diffuse and vague. It loses the ability to inspire; short-term financial targets and crises begin to dominate the agenda, because there is no concept of what is being built in the long term; and the key principles on which decisions are made become blurred. Great leaders leave no ambiguity about what is important. They simplify the message to its elements and they talk about it all the time. That's what Kevin Sheehan did when he took over Norwegian Cruise Line: he reinvigorated his ground staff and onboard crew with a very personal sense of mission.

Several concrete ideas can help leaders to do this better and more often.

Manage the founder's mentality like a key strategic asset. If you agree that the elements of the founder's mentality are as important as we argue in this book, then you should manage that mentality like the strategic asset that it is. Ask yourself whether you are doing this. Go back and look at the agendas of your last five management meetings and last two strategy off-site meetings. Ask when was the last time that you really talked about the differentiation that propels your business model and how you are going to keep it fresh, about what your front-line employees are really saying and feeling, and about how quickly you decide and act relative to outside benchmarks. These simple questions target the strength of the founder's mentality in an organization, and leaders who ask them often discover that the crush of day-to-day concerns has pushed out some of the things that matter the most. Try devoting a half day at your next management off-site meeting to exploring these questions, using data, not opinions. You might be surprised at what you find.

Reach directly down into the organization. The deep concerns of top front-line employees are the best source of raw, current information on customers and often foretell the advent of overload or stall-out. When Tex Gunning, a Dutch CEO who has made a career of leading companies out of difficult crises of growth, took the reins of TNT, a troubled express-package delivery company centered in Europe, he spent the first six weeks at the front lines of the business—in the depots, on the trucks, and with customers. He also sent all seventy thousand of his employees an e-mail soliciting issues, ideas, and concerns. He received over a thousand responses and answered all of them himself. Today, he feels that this was an essential first act: it helped him learn and allowed him to send a signal that the new leadership was going to start by focusing on the front line, not headquarters.

For more than a decade, our own company, Bain & Company, has won awards as the "best place to work" in America. We believe that part of this tracks to how we invest in front-line concerns. For instance, we survey every project team every single month using an online tool and insist that the manager of each team review and act on the results on the spot. The intervention is so valued that we are on the verge of doing this every two weeks and, for some teams, every week. It takes very little time but surfaces issues and concerns instantly, at the point where we can take action. This isn't just a tactic for large companies. We recently shared our Bain survey with See Wai Hun, the founder and CEO of Juris Technologies, a young, fast-growing, financial-software company headquartered in Kuala Lumpur. The next day, she wrote to us to say that the company was already moving toward implementing it—the founder's mentality in action.

No matter how large your company is, go back and look at how you get direct input from employees in the field, with customers, and at production facilities. Are you getting as much as you can from them? Are you using what they tell you? Would they agree with you?

Create a Compass

In 2009, when Paul Polman took over as the CEO of Unilever, he inherited a company in stall-out. Its revenues during the previous decade had declined in a market that was growing fast, its top-four consumer-goods rivals had significantly outperformed it in the stock market, and analysts were describing its previous decade of performance as "purgatory." To turn things around, Polman took a very practical—and necessary—step. He and his top managers created a document called the "Compass," which consisted of a new purpose for the company, a high-level goal, and twelve nonnegotiable principles designed to create more cohesion and reduce complexity. And he used the "Compass" to steer the company back onto the path to scale insurgency.

It wasn't easy. At the time Polman took over, Unilever was huge. Not surprisingly, it was also complex—so much so that it is consistently cited as one of the world's most complex companies. Taking the reins of Unilever in stall-out was therefore a daunting task for Polman, who was the company's first CEO to be hired from the outside. But he took the challenge in stride. "Coming from outside in a very difficult economic environment," he told us, "I had to find a way to be accepted in the company. I did two things. I spent a lot of time studying the values of the company, how it was built. And I had to find a purpose to grow for a company that was not growing. I put the two things together. The purpose of the company has always been to improve people's lives, has always been to make communities in which you operate successful. I said, 'We will create a model where we double our business. While doubling our business, we will reduce our environmental impact and increase societal impact.' I created a strong purpose by putting the best of Unilever together. We changed the compensation system for the longer term and put out some clear signals to tell people that while there might be a crisis, we were investing for the long term."[5]

With a draft version of the "Compass" in hand, Polman and his managers hit the road to hold forums to explain and refine it. When they were done, thousands of employees had participated in the process. They then converted their nonnegotiable principles into plans for action. For instance, they found that a barrier to growth in many regions of the world was talent, yet strategies were approved routinely without a human resource plan. As a result, one of the nonnegotiables stipulated that no strategy would be approved without a detailed human resource plan. Each nonnegotiable had similar measures tying it to the routines of daily life.

Polman has turned Unilever around with great skill. Since he took over, revenues have grown by 22 percent, profits by 60 percent, and the stock price has doubled. Employee engagement across managers is at 75 percent, an all-time high, and in 2014, Unilever was ranked by GlobeScan and SustainAbility as the company doing the most in the world to promote sustainability.[6] Polman connects that achievement directly to a principle set out by William Lever, one of the company's founders, whose core product line consisted of bars of soap designed to improve hygiene during the Victorian era.

Take the time to codify your key principles and use them as a compass to help chart your course. The practice leads to a strong sense of purpose and a powerful consistency of action, and it works for companies of all types and sizes—as we've observed in our studies of Marico, DaVita, Norwegian Cruise Line, IKEA, and LEGO Group.

Essential Decision Skills for the Inner Game of Strategy

Warren Bennis, perhaps the greatest student of leadership, observed that troubled organizations tend to be overmanaged but underled. "The distinction is crucial," he wrote. "Managers are people who do things right, and leaders are people who do the right things. The difference may be summarized as activities of vision and judgment."[7] Bennis goes on to distinguish the *efficiency* of good managers from the *effectiveness* of good leaders, a distinction that we have focused on in our own work on the founder's mentality. Here are a few techniques that make the leaders of scale insurgents so effective.

They Employ Janusian Thinking

Janusian thinking is a term coined by the psychiatrist Albert Rothenberg to denote the creative benefits that can emerge from considering opposites simultaneously. Janus was the Roman god of beginnings and transitions, usually depicted with two faces staring in opposite directions. Some of the world's most creative thinkers, Rothenberg argues, developed their signature ideas in this two-faced way by conceiving of firmly held propositions as "simultaneously true and not true." This can lead to some extraordinarily creative thinking. (Einstein devised his theory of relativity in part by imagining that a man falling from a roof could be at rest and in motion at the same time.)

Simultaneously pursuing the benefits of the founder's mentality *and* the benefits of scale is a classic Janusian endeavor. To create a great insurgency, founders have to ignore industry boundaries and embrace the notion of limitless horizons, but to acquire the benefits of scale they also have to focus tenaciously on the core business and the hard, detailed work of continuous improvement. Both of those things are fundamental to a successful scale insurgency, and they are fundamentally at odds. Likewise, insurgents need to embrace chaos, so that they can mobilize and demobilize resources rapidly to win and maintain customers. But large incumbents derive much of their strength from fixed routines and behaviors, and from riding down the experience curve. The leaders of scale insurgents—companies such as LEGO Group, Yonghui Superstores, Olam International, Haier, Amazon, L Brands, Google, and IKEA—have adopted Janusian ways of thinking about these competing demands, and this allows them to become more than just the sum of their parts. They have managed to forge new amalgams of both scale and speed.

They Say No to Say Yes

One of the true scale insurgents of the finance industry is Vanguard, the investment company founded in 1974 by the legendary investor John Bogle. Bogle founded Vanguard with a simple idea in mind: he believed that small investors could not beat the market in the long term and so based his strategy on the power of indexed stock funds with very low fees. That strategy has propelled Vanguard to become the largest mutual fund company in the world, with $3 trillion of assets under management (making the company now larger than the entire hedge-fund industry). Nonetheless, despite massive temptations to diversify, the company has stayed focused on its core business and core smaller investor customers. We recently asked Bill McNabb, the current CEO, to explain the company's decision-making philosophy to us, and his answer was simple. "Many of the most significant strategic decisions we have made," he said, "have been the decisions to say no to things." The company has turned down all sorts of private equity, real estate, and international ventures simply because they would have distracted Vanguard from its core mission. McNabb told us that the company has even turned down large checks from investors who did not meet their profile, something unheard of in the industry.

The most common strategic root cause of stall-out is the premature abandonment of the core business, or, to put it another way, the inability to say no to new opportunities that don't fit with a company's core mission. Just think of the fifty-six adjacencies in Cisco's portfolio or the loss of focus at Perpetual. Great leaders, we've observed time and again, make clear what a company stands for (its nonnegotiables), because that helps them say no to tempting opportunities that will detract energy or resources from the core. They set the decision-making hurdle very high.

Companies can make it easier to say no in a variety of ways. One is to adopt a philosophy that requires you to kill projects or products at the same rate that you add them. Another is to do what AB InBev does: start the decision-making process by saying no to *everything*, through zero-based budgeting. One of the easiest ways a leader can get in trouble is to adopt the "let a thousand flowers bloom" approach to investing. It won't work, and great founders know it. They know the power of saying no.

They Use the Power of 10X

A few years ago we studied a major European conglomerate with over fifty distinct businesses spread across dozens of markets. The company had experienced no organic growth in over a decade, the stock price had melted away, and it was seeking growth in all the wrong places. We soon realized why. First, the growth of most of its acquisitions (many of them founder-led companies) had actually slowed after being acquired, the opposite of the justification for their purchase, of course. Second, the company's capital was spread uniformly across an extraordinary range of business types and competitive positions. The company was making big bets on its acquisitions, but it had many companies in the family, and it treated them all equally. It invested in its bad businesses hoping that they would become more like the good ones, and it didn't invest hugely in the good ones, because they were doing fine. The result? Consistent mediocrity.

Scale insurgents reject that approach. They are spiky in how they allocate funds and use the power of 10X, by which we mean a willingness to commit ten times the normal resources to a project. For example, Amazon has learned that same-day delivery could increase revenues significantly, and it is also aware that new insurgent start-ups like Instacart and WunWun are focusing on the instant delivery of certain products. So it has invested in its own delivery fleet, drone technology, and more.

The larger a company gets, the smaller it often starts to think when it comes to investments. This process is insidious, and scale insurgents watch out for signs that it is setting in. They always look to make large investments that will best differentiate them in their core. That's how Mukesh Ambani, the wealthiest man in India, has made Reliance Industries, the Mumbai-based industrial giant founded by his father, Dhirubhai Ambani, the most valuable company in India. Guided by a principle he calls the "owner's mentality," which he likens to the founder's mentality, in 2000 Ambani thought big about critical capabilities for the future core of his business and built an integrated petrochemical complex designed to serve a full 25 percent of the giant Indian market, with technology and scale that gave it a 30 percent cost advantage over his regional competitors.[8] Most companies would have backed off from such an investment.

The bottom line: great leaders fight entropy. Be willing to step up to a 10X decision, especially to invest in new assets and capabilities to renew the core.

They Pursue the "Hidden" Root Cause

Great scale insurgents use the founder's mentality to identify problems at their roots and pull them out. Toyota does this with its production system. Whenever workers on the production line see a problem, they immediately set in motion a process of root-cause analysis, sometimes called the "five whys," in which they drill down with a series of "why" questions until they arrive at the real root cause of the problem. We have found that the best leaders intuitively do the same not only for manufacturing problems but also for broader business issues.

Vikram Oberoi is a good example. He once told us how a guest complained on a comment card that her tea was delivered cold. The hotel manager wrote a gracious note of apology to her but didn't investigate the details of the issue, as Vikram discovered when he read the manager's note, called him, and began to probe. (Recall that he is the CEO and has thirty other hotels to worry about.) "The customer was English," Vikram told us, "and I was confident she'd know her tea. So I asked the hotel manager to measure the temperature of the Oberoi hot water against that of a normal tea kettle. And there was a difference. So I asked why that was, and we found that the machines that produced hot water were perceptibly colder toward the end of the descaling cycle. We asked why *that* was and found that we didn't have a standard maintenance program for the machines that took into account the changes in temperature over time. We checked with other Oberoi hotels and realized this was a common problem. We were all delivering slightly cool tea at a certain point in the maintenance cycle. So we solved it. This is how we try to raise our standards every day."

The bottom line: take the extra time and energy to be an active listener. Use the five whys in your business meetings. It might drive those around you crazy, but it will raise the standard of dialogue and increase attention to detail.

They Invest Massively in Next-Generation Leaders

We have never met a leader who felt that he or she had overinvested in talent.

Sunny Verghese, the CEO of Olam, is directly involved in all promotions of his top eight hundred employees, each of whom he knows by name and has an opinion about. Until recently, he insisted on interviewing all hires from the outside—in a company of twenty-three thousand people. AB InBev applies this same level of attention to its hiring. "Talent management," Jo Van Biesbroek told us, "is easily over a third of all executive time when you count it all. It is big." He went on to describe that talent management is especially important because of the uncommonly large jobs and aggressive targets that AB InBev is willing to give to people very early in their careers. "The first time you come in," he said, "you get a hugely difficult target, and we watch for the reaction. You get lots of coaching and guidance, but if you don't embrace challenge, that is a sign. The key element in all of this is how to apply the meritocracy. Everyone talks about it, but our whole system is built on meritocracy. It is why our investment in young talent is so high."

We could go on. The great leaders of scale insurgents invest a huge amount of their time in recruiting talent, mentoring talent, promoting talent, and trying to retain talent. They see clearly that the ability to grow as a company requires the ability to grow their people. Most of these companies have strong biases to promote internally and create lots of general manager and even mini-founder opportunities within the company, to foster responsibility and leadership experiences for their most talented people. The best scale insurgent companies are antibureaucratic and intensely meritocratic. That's because without the right talent, and without a meritocracy to motivate it, companies stop growing.

Consider the following questions: Is the company as much of a meritocracy as it was in its younger days? When was the last time you overrode your human resources systems to reward a true hero of your business, or an extraordinary star? Companies build systems around the averages not the exceptions; sometimes large formal systems need to be overruled.

They Invest Preemptively in Building New Capabilities

Virtually all of the lasting success stories we've explored in this book required a major investment in one or more new capabilities to strengthen or adapt the business model. In the crush of changing the team, redefining and communicating the insurgency, stripping out complexity and cost, and refounding the company internally, it is easy to delay or underinvest in this step. But that would be a mistake. Early in the transformation process, you and your team must ask yourselves what capabilities you need to build or acquire to become fully competitive again.

In her book *The End of Competitive Advantage*, Rita Gunther McGrath argues that any individual advantage in the marketplace today is likely to be fleeting, and that companies therefore need to be constantly investing in their next-generation business model and new capabilities that will differentiate it. Let's illustrate how this works at a company that we know well, and whose ascent to scale insurgency has been based on an ability to constantly build significant new capabilities to push the boundaries out and innovate around its business model. The company is Olam.

From its modest beginnings, in 1989, building a uniquely safe and corruption-proof supply chain to bring cashew nuts from Nigeria, Olam has expanded to forty-five commodities in sixty-five countries, reaching a level of $13.6 billion in annual revenues and more than $650 million in profits. The company's success has made it one of the best-performing IPOs in Asia of the last decade and its CEO, Sunny Verghese, has won many awards, including CEO of the year in Southeast Asia. The company's performance is all the more amazing given the low growth of its markets, the practical challenges of building secure supply chains in places like Nigeria, and the inherent complexity of the business.

Consider this. Before Olam, the typical cashew farmer would sell his crop to a local intermediary, who would then sell the shipment to a distributor, who would then hire someone else to transport the product to warehouses where large global companies would collect it. No one "owned" the full supply chain. As a result, it was leaky, unreliable, hard to trace, and rife with corruption. Farmers received only a tiny fraction of what they were entitled to. Verghese and his team believed that they could differentiate the company to global customers like Nestlé by focusing on the end-to-end supply chain, with the goal of managing the whole thing themselves. Olam succeeded and now has the only supply chain in its key markets that is completely controlled from the farm gate to the end user. Anyone who wants to be a manager at Olam must spend at least three years living in a rural community doing the ground-level work.

Olam is built around four capabilities that differentiate it. Twice a year Verghese takes a week to train personally key managers on what makes Olam special and differentiates its model (built around the most secure supply chains that allow every nut to be tracked back to its origin). The company calls it core process training, and it is a big deal. These sessions ensure that all key employees achieve deep understanding of the handful of capabilities that give Olam competitive advantage. The company is constantly asking itself and acting on this hierarchy of questions we suggest everyone consider for his or her business:

Question: What differentiates the company?

Answer: How we manage supply chains.

Question: How do you do that uniquely?

Answer: By controlling the supply chain from farm gate to customer.

Question: How do you do that uniquely?

Answer: By stationing managers in the rural communities and having a proprietary risk-management system that uses local knowledge to track each product from field to factory.

Question: How do you do *that* uniquely?

Only after that final question do you finally get to the fundamental capabilities at the center of Olam's insurgency now and also in the future. This sequence of questions drives you toward the crown jewels of a business.

Olam's profitable growth, which now spans decades, is a story of reapplying its repeatable model in product after product and country after country. As the company grew, it became expert at adding new capabilities that enabled it to enter new markets and attack nearby profit pools. For instance, the company recognized that secondary processing like sorting, blanching, roasting, packaging, and crushing could be great additions to its supply chain capabilities, doing more of the processing near the origin and delivering a more value-added product to customers. It therefore gained those capabilities, as well as the skill to acquire and integrate local businesses without the need for intermediaries.

We talked earlier about how the great insurgencies are built around the "spikiness" of a few exaggerated strengths. Great companies would rather invest an order of magnitude more than normal, committing the power of 10X to a few deep strengths. Being spiky, not average, is how to win.

We have developed a simple tool for readers to start this discussion. It is a matrix of fifteen basic capabilities and assets that emerged from our analysis of the key differentiators across two hundred businesses and their nine hundred sources of differentiation. You can use the matrix as the starting point to drill down several more levels, like the Olam questions, to the essence of its most important capabilities. (See figure 6-2, which first appeared in our book *Repeatability*.)

Every leadership team—especially those in free fall—should ask the following questions, because, at some point, they will prove to be central to survival:

- What were the strongest capabilities at the core of our past success?
- Are they still relevant and robust?
- What capabilities will we need to compete ("spikiness") in the future?
- How and how much will we invest to acquire these capabilities?

They Shift More Focus to Long-Term Goals and Horizons

Investing preemptively in new capabilities is one of the toughest decisions for a business leader. Why? Because investing requires both cash and expense investments, because it seldom pays off right away, and because, especially in the glare of public market scrutiny, there is seemingly never a good time to do it. The result is a tendency always to be too slow to invest in a major capability, or to try to bootstrap it in a way that never builds the required level of skill fast enough.

But the good news is that there are tactics that leaders can adopt to shift the focus much more toward the long term, which also serve to reinforce the elements of the founder's mentality. Let's look at the example of one founder who has managed this effectively both internally and externally: Robert Keane.

FIGURE 6-2

The capability matrix

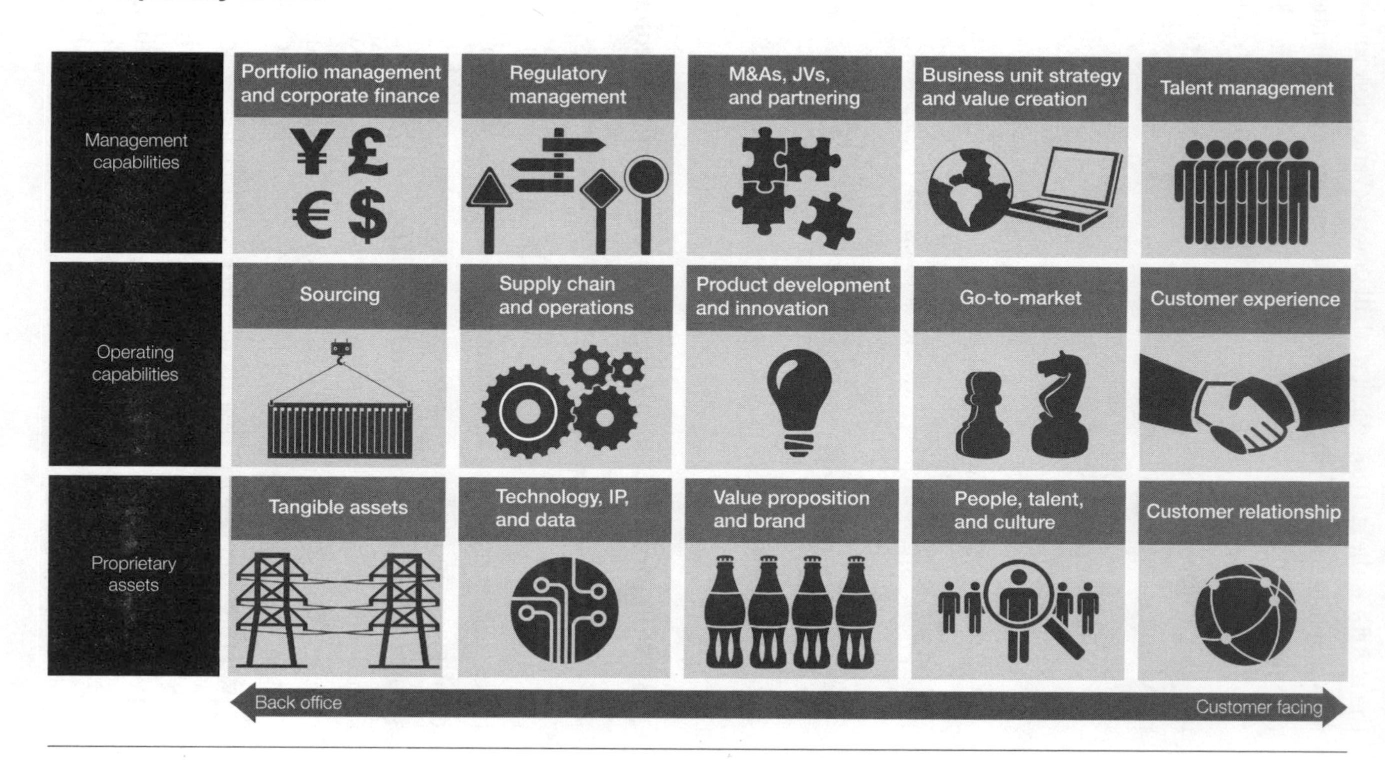

In 1994, Keane founded his company, Cimpress, in a Paris apartment. The idea for the company came to him in the form of an insight that he developed in a class on entrepreneurial ventures at the business school INSEAD. He identified a huge need in micro-businesses for the high-quality printing of everything from business cards to signage, which, he realized, constituted half of the market for commercial printing but did not make much money for the high-volume print shops. Keane developed proprietary practices of what he calls "mass customization" that allowed him to gain economies of scale across the thousands of tiny print orders. His approach, he told us, amounted to "a classic disruptor strategy, starting at the low end of the market that the incumbents were not really pursuing."

It took a while for Cimpress to move from start-up to insurgent, but by 2005, the company had found the formula for its first stage of growth: a repeatable model that allowed it to attack different print segments and different geographies using the Internet for orders, and regional printing facilities with special batching software that enabled mass customization. In 2005, the company hit $90 million in revenues, and by 2011, it had grown by a factor of nearly 10X to more than $800 million. But then overload hit: growth was slowing, margins were compressing, and investors were worrying. "We had a rocket in the right place and right time with a huge cost advantage," Keane said. "We had grown from nothing to $800 million in eight years. But I was worried about signs of slowdown, and even a creeping cancer that stemmed from an insidious cockiness that we could walk on water. We were working very hard but getting physically worn down, and we wondered if we were getting fat and slow. We needed to invest in upgrading our capabilities and in simplifying our business internally, especially how we made decisions. We also decided to start to make some big investments for the long term."

Keane made a number of changes. He wrote a letter to the *Wall Street Journal* announcing that Cimpress was investing for the long term, abandoning annual earnings guidance, and shifting to reward executives and set targets on a longer-term basis. "We clarified the objective to be the world leader in mass customization," he told us, "and to subordinate all financial goals to measures of intrinsic value per share." As part of that effort, Cimpress shifted its focus away from short-term earnings and toward a focus on longer-term return on capital in order to, as Keane put it, "resurrect the entrepreneurial culture, work in teams with long-term goals, and invest to make sure we were lowest cost and fastest in our industry."

This took courage: Keane and his team had to shift their model. They created more business units with clear accountability, even for spending capital. They eliminated all situations where a committee made decisions, creating single decision makers in each unit. They established explicit rules to define the "guard rails" of things like brand management and then let the business operators make the next-level decisions. They shrank corporate functions dramatically and increased the focus of decisions on capital allocation and building long-term capabilities.

The strategy is working. Organic growth at Cimpress has increased in all markets; the company has nearly doubled in size, to $1.5 billion; the mix of investors has shifted to those holding stocks for the longer term. As a result, the stock price has tripled, from $26 in 2011, when these initiatives began, to over $80 in 2015.

The bottom line: recognize the tendency for business goals to become increasingly short term, and fight against that in your capital allocation, internal goals and targets, reward systems, and communications to investors.

They Become the Guardians of Speed and Agility

As organizations grow, they inevitably become more complex and less focused, and they stop growing. This is the paradox of growth. Assemble a thousand human minds in the same building, tell them to simplify something, and they will work hard to make it harder. So leaders must be guardians of speed and agility.

Speed has been a factor in almost every section of this book. Speed to decide. Speed to deliver. Speed to market. Speed to restock inventory. Speed to solve customer problems. Speed to get to the root cause. Speed to adapt. Speed to acquire and integrate. Speed to see crises coming. Speed to prepare. Speed to act. Speed to grow.

Speed wins in most markets today, and scale insurgents know it. Despite their size, the great scale insurgents are among the fastest-moving companies in the world. Research by our colleagues in the organizational practice at Bain & Company shows a tight relationship between company performance, speed of decision, and perceived quality of decisions. Leaders of scale insurgents are acutely aware, we have found, of how their companies can slow down as they grow large. They fight this at every turn by rooting out some or all of the hidden killers of speed on the following list:

Hidden Killers of Speed in Organizations

1. Excess complexity
2. Energy vampires
3. Debates in committees where no person "has the D" (the right to decide)
4. Excessive organizational layers and span breakers

5. Ambiguity around core principles and objectives and a lack of common instincts for how to react to competitors
6. Trapped resources in departments (hence, the power of zero basing)
7. Balkanized customer experiences with no single owner
8. Lack of Monday meetings to de-bottleneck decisions and actions, leaving conflict unresolved
9. Failure to embrace the power of repeatable models so that each new growth opportunity demands new and different capabilities
10. Large corporate staffs endlessly initiating new activities to better inform themselves

The bottom line: leaders should make speed a competitive advantage in everything they do. Every leader should work to reduce the speed killers, promote measures of speed, and encourage new ideas that increase it. In his twenty years as CEO of General Electric, Jack Welch grew the company from $26.8 billion of revenues to almost $130 billion. But he was most known for improving its performance and speed. "When the rate of change inside an institution becomes slower than the rate of change outside," he famously said, "the end is in sight."[9]

But speed isn't enough. Leaders need to be the guardians of agility, too. Throughout the book, we've talked about how CEOs can build more-agile companies. Yonghui, the leading Chinese fresh-food grocer, improves its agility by building insurgent "green store" businesses alongside its incumbent "red store" businesses, figuring that if a new insurgent is going to disrupt its industryes, it should at least be *its* insurgent. The leaders of Mey, the leading spirits player in Turkey, maintain their agility through Monday meetings, which they use to unblock obstacles to innovation and force the sharing of resources—and accountability—across functions and sales territories. AB InBev, for its part, promotes agility by embedding the owner's mindset everywhere in the business.

They Share the Burden of Leadership across the Organization

When we talk about rediscovering the founder's mentality, we don't want readers to conclude that all roads lead back to the CEO. Nor do we want them to conclude that if they want change, they must wait for the CEO to act. No! Our point is just the opposite. If you have embraced the founder's mentality, no matter what your role in a company, you never dismiss a problem as somebody else's. You—and everybody else in the company—own it.

This leads us to the remarkable story of Jabo Floyd.

Floyd, a twenty-five-year veteran of Walmart USA, is the general manager of Distribution Center 6094, in Bentonville, Arkansas. If you want to understand the awesome benefits of size in a company, a Walmart distribution center, or DC, is a good place to start. DCs are testimony to the extraordinary efficiencies that come from scale and from continuous learning that accumulates over decades. Think of a DC as a massive sorting machine. On one side, more than a hundred trucks arrive each day from suppliers, and DC staff people unload their goods. On the other side, nearly two hundred trucks arrive each day from Walmart stores to collect the precise amount of goods needed to restock the shelves in each store. DCs collect no revenue; their performance is measured in terms of efficiency. How fast and accurately are trucks unloaded and loaded at either end of the process? How fast and accurately are goods sorted for the right store? Walmart DCs carry some inventory, but a large volume of the merchandise simply flows from an inbound truck to an outbound truck in a matter of hours.

As one would expect from Walmart, a lot of these efficiencies are realized through the sheer size of the operation. The Bentonville DC runs twenty-four hours a day; trucks arrive and depart from more than three hundred separate dock doors; roughly half a million packages a day travel across 11 miles of conveyor belts; and the trucks leaving the stores travel 1.8 million miles a month to serve the DC's 167 stores. The teams that manage all this movement are headed by tough-minded Walmart veterans with years of experience in leading people to perform at their best. In a business that turns on extraordinary selection and responsiveness to customers, Floyd and his team are franchise players.

Size has its benefits, but as we've discussed in these pages, it can also erode a company's speed and agility. That's a major challenge for Walmart DCs, where balancing the agility-efficiency equation requires continuous improvement. As Walmart broadens the product assortment flowing to DCs, increases the number of smaller-format stores, and builds the capability to deliver packages for both store pickup and home delivery, speed and agility are more important than ever. Growth creates complexity, and complexity kills growth.

Floyd was struggling with the growing complexity of his job when he saw one of our talks about the founder's mentality. Many senior leaders of the company were following the lead of the new CEO, Doug McMillon, who has spoken often about Sam Walton's legacy and the importance of the founder's mentality since taking the job in 2014. The messages have struck a chord. "I've been in the company for twenty-six years," he told us recently, "and I run a business with lots of other tenured veterans of Walmart. These are folks with the gold badges who grew up in the insurgent time of the company. And we've been part of Walmart's incredible growth and movement from insurgent to incumbent. When I saw the presentation on founder's mentality, I said to myself, 'Let's start from today to act as an insurgent. Let's take risks. Let's have fun again. I don't need to wait for someone else to act differently. Let's just start, let's challenge each other, and let's do things differently.'"

In a large company, Floyd observed, it's true that almost everything has been tried before. "It can be stifling," he said, "because anyone can stop a brainstorming session by saying, 'Oh, we did that in 1998, and it didn't work.'" Floyd banned that kind of talk. "The team recognized that we had hit a wall. We needed new ideas and we needed to experiment. We all know we have to do things differently. We're insurgents and we need to experiment. I don't care how we've always done it and I don't care that we tried before and failed. I care about trying and experimenting."

One of the first experiments was changing the way productivity was measured in the DC. "We are very good at measuring each individual to the last detail of performance," Floyd said. "But if an individual gets a bad truck—one that is very hard to unload and sort—their day is ruined. They see the truck and they know they'll never recover for that day. It is soul-destroying." Floyd started to make team performance the prevailing measure. "That way, we all jump in together and deal with the bad trucks, and then we can get on and deal with the easier trucks."

Floyd and his team recognize that they are at the start of a longer journey. The power of the founder's mentality lies partly in the mindset that it fosters as it spreads through an organization. He said,

> I do think there is something in the idea of asking forgiveness, not permission. But experimentation must go hand in hand with a clear understanding of the guard rails. Walmart has this. Our CEO led an effort recently on the

> Walmart "Way of Working." He worked with a lot of us to pool our best thinking about what this means in terms of ethics, of legal standards, of putting the customer first. It is simple and clear. My view is that as long as you are trained on the Walmart "Way of Working" and agree to comply with it, you should be able to experiment within these guidelines. We need to experiment and shake things up.

For Floyd, the benefit of acting like an insurgent is that it unlocks the potential of hundreds of teams working on the front line. "Look, I was a basketball coach," he said, "and for me, it is all about the team. You want everyone to do their best and feel part of winning." As a coach, Floyd didn't want his players looking over at the bench and asking for directions. "I want them to face the opponent and win. Walmart is a team of teams, and if we can unlock the energy of each one but learn from all of them, we'll get the best of insurgency and scale. Sometimes, the muscles that made you famous start to be the ones you stop exercising when you get there. Walmart was built on the energy and teams, and we can get those old muscles back again, while developing the new ones needed to respond to a more complex retail world."

This new team-based orientation has helped with newly recruited associates. "We had a grassroots meeting to talk to our people about how the new team concept was working," Floyd said. "One thing they noted was that this was a big hit with new hires. They now feel they are part of something bigger. They love the idea of being part of a diverse team. They like being teamed with veterans, and the veterans like the energy of new recruits."

Floyd has had one of the more extraordinary careers in business. He started out with one of the great founders in American business, Sam Walton—a true embodiment of the founder's mentality as we've described in this book. And during his career he has become a senior leader at Walmart, helping to make it one of the largest and most successful businesses in American history. But he's not resting on his laurels. Even today, during a time of great turbulence for American retail, he wants Walmart to write the next chapter as a great scale insurgent, and he isn't waiting to start. "I don't want to be the old-school guy," he told us, "the veteran who says we've always done it one way. What keeps me up at night is I wake up and feel that I'm not relevant anymore to the challenges we face. And I don't want the young guys looking at me and saying, 'There's old Jabo, who's done a good job for Walmart for twenty-five years.' I want them to look at me and say, 'There's Jabo who is always trying to shake things up. Jabo is the fresh blood.' I don't want to be the good old guy. I want to be the insurgent."

Floyd's story and his ambitions are profoundly inspiring and a good place to end this book. Floyd has embraced the founder's mentality, as we all can, and now the sky's the limit. Imagine if *you* were the leader in your core business. Imagine if *you* were faster to the ball than anyone in your industry. Imagine if *you* had employees as energized and as committed as Floyd. If you could make that happen, your company would be the best place for the best talent to work, and you would become your competitors' worst nightmare.

You would be a true scale insurgent.

NOTES

All quotes come from author interviews unless otherwise cited.

Introduction

1. Since our first book, *Profit from the Core*, in 2001, we have maintained a database of eight thousand public companies worldwide that we call the "Profit from the Core" database. It now contains thirty years of data, and we use it to analyze patterns of growth around the world; we refer to it as the "actuarial tables" of company growth. Today, worldwide, only about 11 percent of companies have achieved a decade of more than modest sustained and profitable growth that we defined as 5.5 percent revenue and profit growth (currency adjusted), and have also earned their cost of capital. See survey of 377 global executives in survey conducted for Bain & Company by the Economist Intelligence Unit (EIU) in March 2011.

2. Analysis done for our book *Repeatability: Build Enduring Businesses for a World of Constant Change*, based on 300,000 employee surveys that the company Effectory (its business is conducting employee surveys in Europe) analyzed in conjunction with our Bain team.

3. Gallup, *State of the Global Workplace*, 2013.

4. Bain analysis based on data from Capital IQ, company reports, and literature search. Founders index (n = 115) includes companies in the 2014 S&P 500 in which the founder is the CEO or was on the board for at least eight of the past ten years.

5. Bain evaluation of two hundred companies worldwide; internal study relying on literature search and experts.

6. Kevin J. O'Brian, "Nokia's Success Bred Its Weakness: Stifling Bureaucracy Led to Lack of Action on Early Smartphone Innovation," *International Herald Tribune*, September 27, 2010.

7. We examined this with a sample of twenty-five large companies with long histories whose value creation we traced to their beginnings. We then characterized the challenges and decisions facing the company during each period and sorted out the big value swings according to what was happening in the company at the time and its life stage. We found that the large swings in value relative to the stock market averages occurred when the prospects for future profitable growth change up or

down significantly; we also found that these perceptions were related much more to the company performance relative to its industry than industry variations (in fact, over 80 percent of variation in value was within an industry grouping, not relative to the rise and fall of market growth expectations).

8. These estimates came from an analysis that we conducted with our global financial database in which we looked at the speed by which companies were growing as they reached *Fortune* 500 scale. We also used our database of eight thousand global companies over thirty years to look at the fastest-growth companies in the world that have scaled their business to over $10 billion in revenues. We find that companies are able to achieve this several times faster than in past decades. A similar analysis that we conducted ten years ago looked at speed of growth in the 1980s and 1990s, and came to a similar conclusion about the "speed to scale" record holders.

9. "Bain Brief: Strategy Beyond Scale," February 11, 2015.

10. Based on analysis by our Bain team of entrants to and exits from the *Fortune* 500 list of companies from 1994 to 2014. We further validated this by studying the speed of revenue declines of fifty of the largest company stall-outs of the past ten years.

11. Survey of 377 global executives in survey conducted for Bain & Company by the Economist Intelligence Unit (EIU) in March 2011.

Chapter 1

1. Gallup, *State of the Global Workplace*, 2013.

2. This statistic is based on three mutually reinforcing sets of survey results. The first was a survey of Endeavor entrepreneurs at the annual meeting of Endeavor in San Francisco during 2013. The second was a survey of seventy executives, all company founders, in a workshop Chris Zook held in June 2013 at the Vlerick School of Management in Belgium. The third was Bain's Founder's Mentality Global Survey of 325 executives. All showed consistently strong results.

3. Bain evaluation of two hundred companies worldwide.

4. Bain & Company life cycle value analysis in which we took a sample of twenty large, public, global companies and analyzed the major swings in their market value over the course of their history, ascribing each swing to the life cycle period in which it happened, and whether it was in response to its predictable crises.

5. Survey of 377 global executives in survey conducted for Bain & Company by the Economist Intelligence Unit (EIU) in March 2011.

Chapter 2

1. Bain & Company, Stall-Out Analysis, based on eight thousand public companies globally from 1993 through 2013 and a "deep dive" into a sample of fifty large stall-outs to look at causes and the trajectories in more detail.

2. Matthew S. Olson, Derek van Bever, and Seth Verry, "When Growth Stalls," *Harvard Business Review*, March 2008.

3. Survey of 377 executives in North America, Western Europe, and Asia conducted jointly by Bain and EIU, March 2011.

4. Bain & Company analysis of fifty significant business transformations.

5. Bain analysis in which we took a sample of fifty industrial classifications (like public utilities or airlines) and worked with internal experts to identify the number of ways that the industry at the time was undergoing major turbulence (such as deregulation of the airlines or new pricing models like energy exchanges) or not.

6. John Kador, *Charles Schwab: How One Company Beat Wall Street and Reinvented the Brokerage Industry* (Hoboken, NJ: John Wiley & Sons, 2002).

7. Net Promoter Score is a measure of customer advocacy developed by Fred Reichheld, who showed a strong relationship between the score and the ability of a business to achieve profitable growth. It is a simple index based on asking customers to rate on a scale of 1 to 10 their inclination to recommend the product or service to a friend. The index is calculated by subtracting the percent of customers who are "detractors" (those giving only a rating of 0 to 6) from the percentage who are "promoters" (those giving a rating of 9 or 10). We looked at this index across a range of industries and company sizes and found a strong negative relationship between scale and Net Promoter Scores on average. Yet, in every category, there were always a few outliers of large companies that had maintained customer advocacy, even at large size, because of what they had done to maintain the founder's mentality and to avoid balkanization of the experience.

8. Clayton Christensen, *The Innovator's Dilemma* (Boston: Harvard Business Press, 1997).

9. Bain, Founder's Mentality survey of 325 executives worldwide, September 2013.

10. Michael Mankins, Bain Brief: "This weekly meeting took up to 300,000 hours a year," April 2014.

11. Temkin Group, "Employee Engagement Benchmark Survey," January 2012.

12. David Packard, *The HP Way: How Bill Hewlett and I Built Our Company* (New York: HarperCollins, 2006).

13. A Letter from Walter Hewlett, *Wall Street Journal*, February 13, 2002.

14. Bill Taylor, "How Hewlett-Packard Lost the HP Way," *Harvard Business Review*, September 23, 2011.

Chapter 3

1. See the blogs at www.foundersmentality.com website for a wide range of ideas on overriding systems.

Chapter 4

1. First estimated in Matthew S. Olson and Derek van Bever, *Stall Points* (New Haven, CT: Yale University Press, 2008), and verified by recent Bain & Company analysis showing that the risk and severity of stall-outs is increasing.

2. Niall Ferguson, "Complexity and Collapse," *Foreign Affairs*, March 2010.

Chapter 5

1. David C. Robertson with Bill Breen, *Brick by Brick* (New York: Crown Business, 2013).

Chapter 6

1. Arthur Blank and Bernie Marcus with Bob Andelman, *Built from Scratch: How a Couple of Regular Guys Grew The Home Depot from Nothing to $30 Billion* (New York: Crown Business, 1999), xvii.

2. Sam Walton with John Huey, *Sam Walton: Made in America* (New York: Doubleday, 1992).

3. Ray Kroc with Robert Anderson, *Grinding It Out: The Making of McDonald's* (Chicago, IL: Contemporary Books, 1985).

4. Andrew S. Grove, *Only the Paranoid Survive: How to Exploit the Crisis Points That Challenge Every Company* (New York: Currency, 1996).

5. Vinod Mahanta and Priyanka Sangani, "Corporate Dossier," *Economic Times of India*, November 9, 2013.

6. Unilever, https://www.unilever.com/sustainable-living/the-sustainable-living-plan/our-strategy/awards-and-recognition/.

7. Warren Bennis and Burt Nanus, *Leaders: Strategies for Taking Charge* (New York: Harper & Row Publishers, 1985).

8. Hamish McDonald, *The Polyester Prince: The Rise of Dhirubhai Ambani* (New South Wales, Australia: Allen and Unwin Pty. Limited, 1999).

9. Vikram Oberoi, interview.

10. GE Annual Report, 2000.

BIBLIOGRAPHY

Books

Bennis, Warren G., and Patricia Ward Biederman. *Organizing Genius: The Secrets of Creative Collaboration*. New York: Perseus Books, 1997.

Bhat, Harish. *Tata Log: Eight Modern Stories from a Timeless Institution*. New York: Random House Penguin, 2012.

Carnegie, Andrew. *The Autobiography of Andrew Carnegie*. New York: Signet Classics, 2006.

Chernow, Ron. *Titan: The Life of John D. Rockefeller, Sr.* New York: Vintage Books, 1998.

Christensen, Clayton M. *The Innovator's Dilemma: When New Technologies Cause Great Firms to Fail*. Boston: Harvard Business School Press, 1997.

Collins, James C., and Jerry I. Porras. *Built to Last: Successful Habits of Visionary Companies*. New York: HarperBusiness, 1997.

Cord, David J. *The Decline and Fall of Nokia*. Helsinki: Schildts & Söderströms, 2014.

Dell, Michael, with Catherine Fredman. *Direct from Dell: Strategies That Revolutionized an Industry*. New York: HarperBusiness, 1999.

DeRose, Chris, and Noel Tichy. *Judgment at the Front Line*. New York: Portfolio Penguin, 2012.

Fischer, Bill, Umberto Lago, and Fang Liu. *Reinventing Giants: How Chinese Global Competitor Haier Has Changed the Way Big Companies Transform*. San Francisco: Jossey-Bass, 2013.

Gallo, Carmine. *The Innovation Secrets of Steve Jobs: Insanely Different Principles for Breakthrough Success*. New York: McGraw-Hill, 2010.

Goodheart, Adam. *1861: The Civil War Awakening*. New York: Vintage Books, 2011.

Greenberg, Maurice R., and Lawrence A. Cunningham. *The AIG Story*. Hoboken, NJ: John Wiley & Sons, 2013.

Grove, Andy. *Only the Paranoid Survive*. New York: Bantam Doubleday Dell Publishing Group, 1996.

Guaracy, Thales. *O Sonho Brasileiro: Como Rolim Adolfo Amaro Construiu a TAM e Sua Filosofia de Negocios* Portuguese ed. editoracopacabana, 2003.

Horowitz, Ben. *The Hard Thing about Hard Things: Building a Business When There Are No Easy Answers.* New York: HarperCollins Publishers, 2014.

Hsieh, Tony. *Delivering on Happiness.* New York: Business Plus-Hachette Group, 2010.

Isaacson, Walter. *Steve Jobs.* New York: Simon & Schuster, 2011.

Janis, Irving L. *Groupthink: Psychological Studies of Policy Decisions and Fiascoes.* Boston: Houghton-Mifflin, 1982.

Kador, John. *Charles Schwab: How One Company Beat Wall Street and Reinvented the Brokerage Industry.* Hoboken, NJ: John Wiley & Sons, 2002.

Kahneman, Daniel. *Thinking, Fast and Slow.* New York: Farrar, Straus and Giroux, 2011.

Kaku, Michio. *The Future of the Mind.* New York: Random House, 2014.

Karkara, Bachi J. *Dare to Dream: A Life of M.S. Oberoi.* New Delhi, India: Portfolio Penguin, 1993.

Kiechel, Walter. *The Lords of Strategy.* Boston: Harvard Business Press, 2010.

Lala, R. M. *For the Love of India: The Life and Times of Jamsetji Tata.* New Delhi, India: Portfolio Penguin, 2004.

Larish, John J. *Out of Focus: The Story of How Kodak Lost Direction.* Privately published, 2012.

Lashinsky, Adam. *Inside Apple.* New York: Business Plus, 2013.

Levy, Steven. *In the Plex: How Google Thinks, Works, and Shapes Our Lives.* New York: Simon & Schuster, 2011.

Lumet, Sidney. *Making Movies.* New York: Vintage Books, 1996.

McDonald, Hamish. *Mahabharata in Polyester.* New South Wales: New South Wales Press, 2010.

Marcus, Bernie, and Arthur Blank. *Built from Scratch.* New York: Crown Business, 1999.

Mondavi, Robert. *Harvests of Joy.* New York: Harcourt, Inc., 1998.

Olson, Matthew S., and Derek van Bever. *Stall Points.* New Haven, CT: Yale University Press, 2008.

Packard, David. *The HP Way: How Bill Hewlett and I Built Our Company.* New York: Harper Collins, 1995.

Pink, Daniel H. *Drive: The Surprising Truth about What Motivates Us.* Edinburgh, Scotland: Rivergate Books, 2009.

Reichheld, Fred. *The Ultimate Question 2.0: How Net Promoter Companies Thrive in a Customer-Driven World.* Boston: Harvard Business School Press, 2011.

Ries, Eric. *The Lean Start-Up: How Today's Entrepreneurs Use Continuous Innovation to Create Radically Successful Businesses.* New York: Crown Business, 2011.

Robertson, David, and Bill Green. *Brick by Brick: How LEGO Rewrote the Rules of Innovation and Conquered the Global Toy Industry.* New York: Crown Business, 2013.

Rottenberg, Linda. *Crazy Is a Complement: The Power of Zigging over Zagging.* New York: Portfolio Penguin, 2014.

Schelling, Thomas C. *Micromotives and Macrobehavior.* New York: WW Norton, 1978.

Schmidt, Eric, and Jonathan Rosenbert. *How Google Works.* New York: Grand Central Publishing, 2013.

Schultz, Howard. *Onward: How Starbucks Fought for Its Life Without Losing Its Soul.* New York: Rodale Press, 2010.

Sheehy, Gail. *New Passages: Mapping Your Life Across Time.* New York: Random House, 1995.

Shelp, Ron. *Fallen Giant: The Amazing Story of Hank Greenberg and the History of AIG.* Hoboken, NJ: John Wiley & Sons, 2009.

Simon, Hermann. *Hidden Champions of the 21st Century: Success Strategies of Unknown World Market Leaders.* New York: Springer, 2009.

Snyder, Paul. *Is This Something George Eastman Would Have Done?* Rochester, NY: Privately published, 2013.

Stadler, Christian. *Enduring Success: What We Can Learn from the History of Outstanding Corporations.* Stanford, CA: Stanford Business Books, 2011.

Stiles, T. J. *The First Tycoon: The Epic Life of Cornelius Vanderbilt.* New York: Knopf Doubleday, 2009.

Stone, Brad. *The Everything Store: Jeff Bezos and the Age of Amazon.* London: Bantam Press, 2013.

Syed, Matthew. *Bounce: How Champions Are Made.* London: Fourth Estate, 2010.

Thiel, Peter, and Blake Masters. *Zero to One: Notes on Startups, or How to Build the Future.* New York: Crown Publishing, 2014.

Wallace, James, and James Erikson. *Hard Drive: Bill Gates and the Making of the Microsoft Empire.* New York: Harper Collins, 1992.

Wolcott, Robert C., and Michael Lippitz. *Grow from Within.* New York: McGraw Hill, 2010.

Zook, Chris. *Beyond the Core: Expand Your Market Without Abandoning Your Roots.* Boston: Harvard Business School Press, 2004.

———. *Profit from the Core: A Return to Growth in Turbulent Times. With James Allen.* Boston: Harvard Business Press, 2010.

———. *Unstoppable: Finding Hidden Assets to Renew the Core and Fuel Profitable Growth*. Boston: Harvard Business School Press, 2007.

Zook, Chris, and James Allen. *Repeatability: Build Enduring Businesses for a World of Constant Change*. Boston: Harvard Business Review Press, 2012.

Articles

Allen, James, Dunigan O'Keeffe, and Chris Zook. "Founder's Mentality: The Paths to Great Repeatable Models." Bain & Company, Boston, May 3, 2013.

Blenko, Marcia, Eric Garton, Ludovica Mottura, and Oliver Wright. "Winning Operating Models That Convert Strategy to Results." Bain & Company, Boston, 2014.

Bloch, Nicolas, James Hadley, Ouriel Lancry, and Jenny Lundqvist. "Strategy beyond Scale." Bain & Company, Boston, 2015.

Cassano, Erik. "Medicine Man: How Kent Thiry Cured DaVita Inc. of Its Ills and Turned It into an Industry Leader." *SmartBusiness*, January 2007.

"Charles Schwab: Return of the King." *The Economist*, July 22, 2004.

Dyer, Jeffrey H., Hal B. Gregersen, and Clayton M. Christensen. "The Innovator's DNA." *Harvard Business Review*, December 2009.

Fahlenbrach, Rudiger. "Founder-CEOs, Investment Decisions, and Stock Market Performance." Working paper, Ohio State University, Fisher College of Business, August 8, 2007.

"Founder Returns Charles Schwab to Its Maverick Roots." *MarketWatch*, December 6, 2005.

Groom, Nichola. "Schultz Back as Starbucks CEO; US Expansion Slowed." Reuters News, January 7, 2008.

Hansen, Morten T., Herminia Ibarra, and Urs Peyer. "The Best-Performing CEOs in the World." *Harvard Business Review*, January-February 2013.

Hewlett, Walter. "Letter to Hewlett Packard Shareholders." *Wall Street Journal*, February 13, 2002.

Hjelmgaard, Kim. "Back from the Brick: How LEGO Was Transformed." *MarketWatch*, December 23, 2009.

Iansiti, Marco, and Roy Levien. "Strategy as Ecology." *Harvard Business Review*, March 2004.

Ignatius, Adi. "The HBR Interview: 'We Had to Own the Mistakes.'" *Harvard Business Review, July-August 2010*.

Jones, Del, and Matt Krantz. "Firms, Investors Tend to Prosper with Founders at Helm." *USA Today*, August 22, 2007.

Kedrosky, Paul. "The Constant: Companies That Matter." Ewing Marion Kauffman Foundation, May 2013.

Laurie, Donald L., and J. Bruce Harreld. "Six Ways to Sink a Growth Initiative." *Harvard Business Review,* July-August 2013.

Mankins, Michael C., and Richard Steele. "Turning Great Strategy into Great Performance." *Harvard Business Review,* July-August 2005.

Martens, Martin L. "Hang On to Those Founders." *Harvard Business Review,* October 1, 2005.

Morris, Betsy. "Steve Jobs Speaks Out." *Fortune,* March 7, 2008.

Nakamura, Noriko, and Mayumi Negishi. "Sharp's New Boss Says It Suffers From 'Big Company Disease.'" *Wall Street Journal* blog, blogs.wsj.com/japanrealtime/2013/06/25.

O'Brien, Kevin J. "Nokia's Success Bred Its Weakness; Stifling Bureaucracy Led to Lack of Action on Early Smartphone Innovation." *International Herald Tribune,* September 27, 2010.

Olson, Matthew S., Derek van Bever, and Seth Verry. "When Growth Stalls." *Harvard Business Review,* March 2008.

Porter, Michael E. "What Is Strategy?" *Harvard Business Review, November-December 1996.*

Schein, Edgar H. "The Role of the Founder in Creating Organizational Culture." *Organizational Dynamics,* Summer 1983.

Strangler, Dane, and Robert E. Litan. "Where Will the Jobs Come From?" *Firm Formation and Economic Growth.* Kauffman Foundation Research Series, November 2009.

Taylor, Bill. "How Hewlett-Packard Lost the HP Way." *Harvard Business Review,* September 23, 2011.

Wasserman, Noam. "The Founder's Dilemma." *Harvard Business Review,* February 2008.

Wats, Robert. "The Good Brick Who Rebuilt LEGO." *Telegraph,* December 17, 2006.

Zook, Chris, and James Allen. "The Great Repeatable Business Model." *Harvard Business Review,* November 2011.

INDEX

ACKNOWLEDGMENTS

When we look back on the years of work that went into *The Founder's Mentality* we are struck by the large number of amazing people who devoted their time, their expertise, and their insights to this project. As authors we are humbled and grateful.

Well over a hundred executives, most of them busy CEOs and founders of companies, devoted countless hours sharing with us their stories, the challenges they faced along the way, and the best techniques they used to surmount those challenges and create enduring companies. Their stories and insights from the front lines of business are at the core of this book. We completed this project with the highest level of respect for what such business leaders, and especially founders, have accomplished during their lives, and for the skill and willpower that enabled their successes.

Our partners at Bain & Company were constantly supportive of our effort and responded generously and quickly to our requests for references, case examples, critiques, and ideas. During the course of writing *The Founder's Mentality*, we delivered literally hundreds of workshops, talks, and presentations to the clients of our partners, allowing us to apply our ideas at the coal face of business as well as to constantly learn and pressure-test improvements. We feel incredibly lucky to have worked with such a generous and capable group of people willing to share so selflessly. We would especially like to thank Nicolas Bloch, Stefano Bridelli, Innocent Dutiro, François Faelli, Toshi Hiura, Dunigan O'Keeffe, Charles Ormiston, Raj Pherwani, and Steve Schaubert. Steve suffered an untimely death just months before the completion of this book.

He remains in our memories and at the top of the list of those to whom we are most grateful for his sage advice on our books as well as for the way in which he role modeled the founder's mentality.

Bain & Company allowed us to work with some truly all-star consultants and analysts to help us figure out everything from the stall-out rates of companies to the odds of sustaining profitable growth. We would especially like to thank the leaders of these research efforts: Sonal Pruthi, Bhavya Nand Kishore, Anouk Piening, Alice Leonard, Lucy Cummings, Jennifer Kim, and Ashleigh Sullivan. You are the best of the brightest. Ralph D'Angelo was our go-to library whiz for the toughest searches. Brenda Davis, Chris's assistant of over twenty years, kept us organized and provided positive karma all along the way.

We thank editorial director Tim Sullivan, senior editor Melinda Merino, and the remarkable team they assembled at Harvard Business Review Press, from cover design to technical editing and production. Thank you for taking on this project and making it one of Harvard's featured books of this year.

Rafe Sagalyn, our agent, went above and beyond, suggesting some changes in the organization of the book and finding an experienced editor, Toby Lester, to sharpen our prose. Toby's keystrokes are evident on nearly every page. Thank you, Toby.

The Bain & Company marketing team, led by Wendy Miller and Paul Judge, was tireless in helping us with issues from writing style to editorial issues and even the use of track change software (which constantly stymied us), yet we never exceeded the amazing limits of their patience and knowledge. One of the real stars of the show was Maggie Locher, who was the "keeper of the master" at critical times in the voyage as well as the person who undertook the detailed process of fact-checking. If anything slipped through, it is our fault, but the level of attention and precision Maggie brought to the task was Herculean.

Finally, we offer our deepest thanks to Donna Robinson and Kathy Allen, our understanding wives, for putting up with endless family schedule disruptions and distracted partners while unfailingly offering support, sage advice, and positive energy, all of which we needed in abundance.

ABOUT THE AUTHORS

Chris Zook is a partner at Bain & Company and was a coleader of the firm's Global Strategy practice for twenty years. The *Times* (London) has named him one of the world's fifty most-influential global business thinkers.

In his work with clients, Zook focuses on helping companies find their next wave of profitable growth. He has worked in a range of industries, including information, health care, computers, and venture capital. He is a frequent speaker at global forums, including the World Economic Forum at Davos.

Zook is the author of the bestselling books *Profit from the Core, Beyond the Core, Repeatability*, and *Unstoppable*, published by Harvard Business Review Press, and has written extensively for publications such as the *Wall Street Journal* and the *Washington Post*. He has been a guest on NPR, CNBC, and Bloomberg TV and is a frequent speaker at a wide range of business forums, including the Forbes Global CEO Conference, the BusinessWeek CEO Summit, the Economist Summit, and the Harvard Distinguished Speaker Series.

A graduate of Williams College with advanced degrees in economics from Exeter College, Oxford University, and Harvard University, Zook has a wife and family and divides his time between homes in Amsterdam and Boston.

James Allen is a partner in Bain & Company's London office and a coleader of Bain's Global Strategy practice. He has served in a variety of leadership roles at Bain and is the founder of the

Bain Founder's Mentality 100, a global network of high-growth companies mostly led by their founders.

Allen has more than twenty-five years of consulting experience and has worked extensively for global companies in consumer products, oil and gas, technology and telecommunications, health care, and other industries. He has advised clients on the development of global growth strategies, emerging market entry strategies, and turnaround strategies.

Allen is a coauthor of the bestselling books *Profit from the Core* and *Repeatability* and has written numerous articles on the topics of growth strategy, customer strategy, and the consumer of 2020. He is a frequent speaker at the World Economic Forum and other conferences and has been writing for Bain's *The Founder's Mentality* blog for the last three years.

A graduate of Kenyon College, Johns Hopkins School of Advanced International Studies, and Harvard Business School, Allen lives in London with his wife and their three children.